THE INDIE FOLK
GUITAR BOOK

Discover Altered Tunings, Fingerpicking and Creative Acoustic Guitar Techniques

STUART**RYAN**

FUNDAMENTAL**CHANGES**

The Indie Folk Guitar Book

Discover Altered Tunings, Fingerpicking and Creative Acoustic Guitar Techniques

ISBN: 978-1-78933-447-0

Published by **www.fundamental-changes.com**

Copyright © 2024 Stuart Ryan

Edited by Joseph Alexander & Tim Pettingale

The moral right of this author has been asserted.

www.fundamental-changes.com

For over 350 free guitar lessons with videos check out:

www.fundamental-changes.com

Join our free Facebook Community of Cool Musicians

www.facebook.com/groups/fundamentalguitar

Tag us for a share on Instagram: **FundamentalChanges**

Cover Image Copyright: Shutterstock, Theeradech Sanin

Contents

Introduction

Indie-folk is a genre in which you'll find a multitude of artists who approach the guitar from their own unique perspectives, and it offers plenty of inspiration to fuel your own playing style. While you won't find screaming leads or 1/32nd note sweep picking here, it's a mistake to assume that these players eschew technique. In fact, you'll find articulate fingerpicking, complex chords, melodic lines, and much more.

At the heart of the genre, however, is *texture*. Even though the guitar usually plays a supporting role to the voice, it often expresses complex harmony or plaintive, effects-laden ideas that create a rich tapestry of sound. By using detailed fingerpicking parts and altered tunings, the guitar becomes a voice of its own, and many accompanying parts are strong enough to stand on their own as instrumental ideas.

In this book you'll learn the techniques and approaches that indie-folk guitarists use – all of which you'll be able to take into other genres. You'll discover how the fingerpickers create challenging patterns that dance across the strings; you'll learn how simple harmonies like tenths can be used to create evocative yet spare accompaniments; and how altered tunings are used to access voicings and textures that can't be created in standard tuning. Some parts feature electric guitars, while others examine the role of the acoustic. When you've got the foundations in place, you'll learn how individual artists have developed their own fascinating idiosyncrasies and, finally, you'll put everything into practice in beautiful full performance pieces with a band.

The indie-folk scene has grown dramatically in the last twenty years, with bands like Mumford and Sons taking the genre into the mainstream. By the end of this book, you'll find yourself to be a more creative guitarist with a whole new style and playlist to explore!

Have fun and, as ever, get in touch with any questions.

Stu.

Get the Audio

The audio files for this book are available to download for free from **www.fundamental-changes.com.** The link is in the top right-hand corner. Click on the "Guitar" link then simply select this book title from the drop-down menu and follow the instructions to get the audio.

We recommend that you download the files directly to your computer, not to your tablet, and extract them there before adding them to your media library.

For over 350 free guitar lessons with videos check out:

www.fundamental-changes.com

Join our free Facebook Community of Cool Musicians

www.facebook.com/groups/fundamentalguitar

Tag us for a share on Instagram: FundamentalChanges

Chapter One – Fingerpicking Fundamentals

Fingerpicking is integral to indie-folk, so let's begin with a primer on this essential technique, just in case your fingers need a refresher or a bit of refinement.

Traditional folk fingerpickers like Bob Dylan and Paul Simon take a quasi-classical approach. This means using your thumb to play the low E, A and D strings, then using your first finger on the G string, second finger on the B string, and third finger on the high E string. You'll also see this approach in the classically-tinged playing of modern artists like Jose Gonzales.

Some players don't use their third finger at all, instead relying on the first and second fingers to cover the G, B and E strings. Others take a more idiosyncratic approach, using just the thumb and first finger, but it's usually possible to play their parts with a more classically "correct" technique if desired.

Let's start with some basic picking patterns to help get your technique consistent before we move on to some more complex and challenging ideas. In the later examples I'll label any unusual finger combinations using the standard PIMA notation:

p = Thumb

i = Index/first finger

m = Middle/second finger

a = Anular/third finger

Begin with a relaxed picking hand and a loose, slightly bent wrist. Place your thumb on the low E string with your first finger on the G string, second finger on the B string, and first finger on the high E string. Pick the low E string with a downward "push" of your thumb, followed by the same on the A and D strings, then play the G, B and D strings with an upward stroke of each finger.

Example 1a

Now the pattern is reversed. Orient your picking hand with the fingers planted on the strings as before and play the exercise. When you have played this a few times, play the pattern again with your fingers floating slightly above each string before you strike them, instead of planting them.

Example 1b

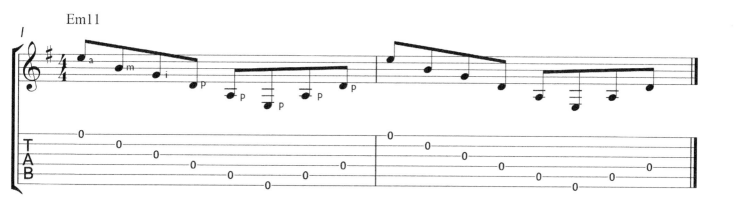

The next pattern teaches you to isolate your thumb and fingers to build your finger independence. Here, your fingers will roll down the strings starting with a different bass note each time. Listen carefully to each string to hear whether you are creating an even volume or if your thumb/bass notes overpower the other strings. Are the G, B and E strings loud enough against the bass?

Example 1c

Next is an important bass-note-then-chord pattern. The thumb strikes the bass notes as before but there are now two options to play the G, B, and E strings together. You can pluck them with your first, second and third fingers to create a very clean sound. However, you can strike the three strings with a downstroke with your first finger nail, or brush the strings with the nails on your first, second and third fingers to give a more percussive sound.

Example 1d

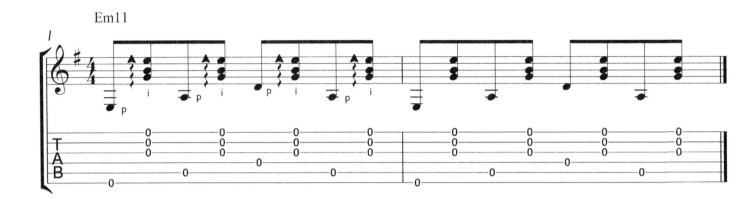

Let's add some chord shapes. This pattern features a roll down the strings and the bass/chord approach from above. On beat 1, either play the A and D strings with your thumb followed by your first and second fingers, or use your thumb on the A string, then one finger per string. Reverse these patterns in bar two.

Example 1e

Now we move to a G major chord but stick to the technique of the previous example. If you are playing the low E string and D strings with the picking hand thumb, you'll feel the distance between these two strings. This is great practice for the alternating bassline patterns which follow.

Example 1f

Here the bassline alternates between the A and E strings. For stability, I suggest using your thumb for the E, A, and D strings, and your first, second and third fingers for the G, B and E strings. The fingers can pluck these strings or use a downward brushing motion. Be consistent with whichever pattern you are working with.

Example 1g

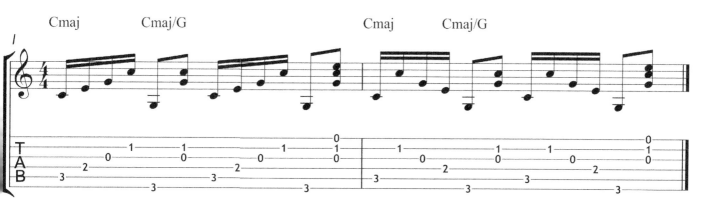

The bassline moves from the E to A strings here, and in this exercise I want you to explore the dynamic range of the picking hand. Strike some strings harder and see how much volume you can produce. Then contrast this with a lighter touch on other strings. Varied dynamics are a huge part of this style, so spend time playing with these exercises to see how much difference you can create between loud and soft.

Example 1h

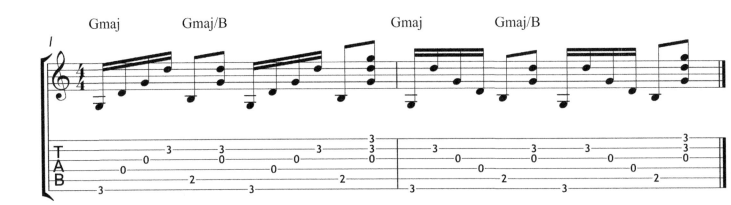

This example introduces two important concepts. The first is syncopation (playing notes off the beat). This happens here when you play the open G string on the "&" of beats 2 and 4 (counting the bar in 1/8th notes i.e., "1 & 2 & 3 & 4 &"). This is a great exercise for time keeping, so ensure you are counting the beats. We're also introducing the richer sounds of sus4 and major 9 chords, which we'll use again later.

Example 1i

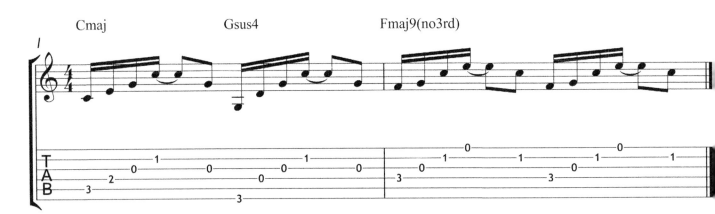

Embellishing chords with hammer-ons quickly turns these exercises into more musical ideas. In each chord, your third finger is on the 3rd fret, your first finger on 1st fret, and your second plays each hammer-on to the 2nd fret. Keep the fretting hand fingers in place throughout, so that all the notes ring together.

Example 1j

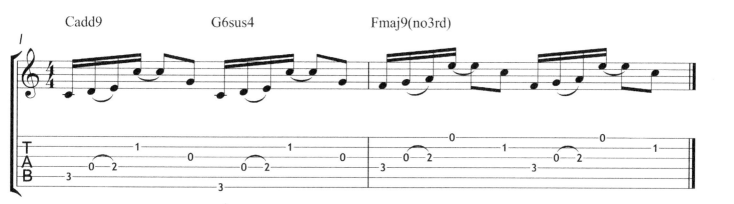

Here, the picking-hand fingerings follow the structure you learned earlier, but now you must ensure your thumb and second finger pluck two strings simultaneously with even dynamics. The low E and A strings are louder than the B string, so dig in with that second finger!

Example 1k

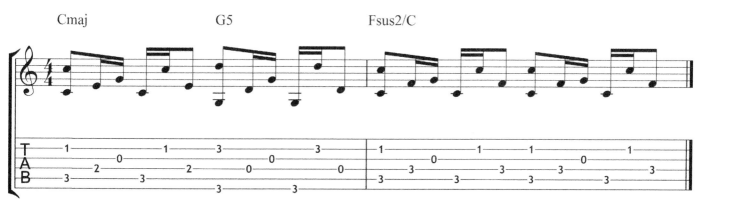

This classic folk fingerpicking pattern features a descending bassline. Start with an open C major chord shape. In bar two, keep your first finger on the 1st fret of the B string and hook your thumb over to the 1st fret of the low E string.

Example 1l

Moving notes within chord shapes is a device used by many indie-folk artists. This C major chord has a note moving on the B string, so use your fourth finger to play the note on the 3rd fret. The challenge is to coordinate this movement with the picking hand pattern and keep all the fingers on the strings throughout.

Example 1m

In this example we move from the I chord (C) to the V chord (G) while keeping the same picking pattern. Many artists don't consciously hunt for chords like this G6sus4 – they are just the result of moving over the idea from the C chord in bar one.

Example 1n

In this G Major progression, the open strings are used to add character to basic major chords, so the D major features an open B string to add a sixth, and the C major has an open D string turning it into a Csus2.

Example 1o

This progression fingerpicks through a I ii vi IV progression (G – Am7 – Em – Csus2). As you'll discover later, many players use a capo so that they can maintain the shapes and patterns they are used to from the open position in other keys. The chords themselves are often subtly altered from basic major chords to sus2, sus4 and add9 voicings for a richer sound.

As most indie-folk involves accompanying singer-songwriter style music, it's a good idea to practice playing through common chord progressions in all keys.

Example 1p

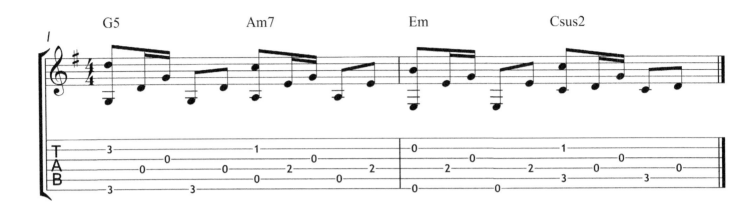

Now let's work through a I V vi IV progression (G – D – Em – C). The chords change more rapidly here, and you'll find an alternate voicing for a Csus2 in bar two. This time the sus2 (D) is played as both the open D string and at the 3rd fret of the B string. You'll find this common indie-folk chord shape all over the place!

Example 1q

We don't always have to start on the I chord, of course, and in this example the progression is ii V I IV (Am – D – G – C). As with the previous examples, listen out for the colour in the chords, especially the D6/F# and the moving melody note on the B string in bar two.

Example 1r

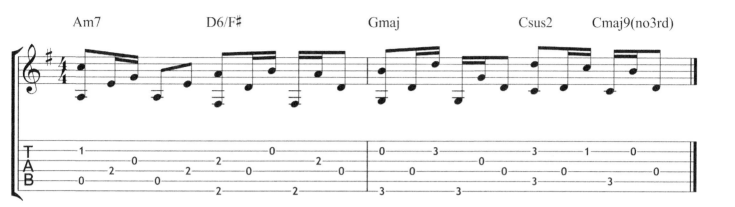

This longer example demonstrates how we can move notes to create rich sounding chords.

Use your fourth finger to play the moving notes on the B string. In bar two, remove your second finger from the 2nd fret of the D string. Your third finger moves the bassline from the 3rd fret of the A string to the low E string. In bars three and four, use your second finger on the 3rd fret of the A string, and your third finger for the 3rd fret of the D string. The first and fourth fingers are used on the B string as before.

Example 1s

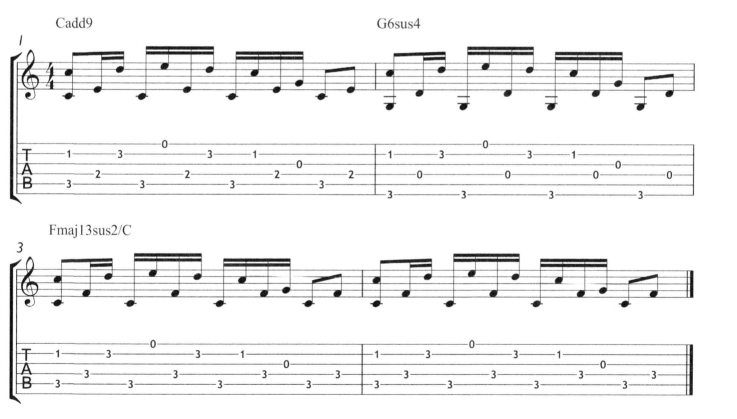

Chapter Two – Understanding Altered Tunings

Altered tunings are a big part of indie-folk guitar, but figuring out how they work can be daunting. In this chapter you'll learn how to approach these tunings methodically, so you can find your way around any you encounter.

Some altered tunings are only a small departure from standard tuning. For example, Drop D, where the low E string is lowered a tone to D, or Double Drop D, where both E strings are tuned down a tone.

Some, like Open D (DADF#AD) or the popular DADGAD, are more self-contained.

Explore further, however, and you'll start to discover the low resonance of tunings like CADGAD or CGDGCD.

Finally, some artists (I'm looking at you Nick Drake!) have created bespoke tunings that seemingly have little logic, but offer magnificent chords, harmonies and compositional possibilities.

Ideally, you should stick to any new tuning for a while and develop a decent map of the fretboard, so that you know where the notes are located and can play a range of scales and chords.

DADGAD Tuning

DADGAD is the first altered tuning many guitarists explore. It's said that folk guitarist Davey Graham created this tuning to emulate the sound of Middle Eastern instruments like the Oud. It reached a wider audience via Jimmy Page and quickly became the *de facto* folk tuning. The notes DADGAD spell out a Dsus4 chord, so it is neither major nor minor. We can, however, play plenty of major and minor chords within it.

A fantastic tip is to approach any altered tuning by first mapping out all the tenth intervals (a third played an octave above the root). This effectively gets you playing simple major and minor chords up the neck and stops you from getting stuck in the open position.

Example 2a

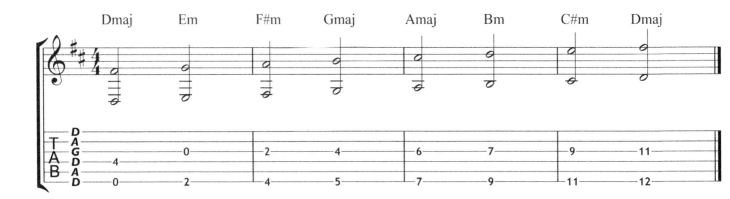

Adding open strings to these tenth intervals quickly allows musical ideas to emerge from the tuning. This approach is taken by Laura Marling and Mumford and Sons, along with many more indie-folk artists, and is an effective way to create some beautiful ideas very quickly. When you can play this example, try adding different open strings and change the rhythm to create parts of your own.

Example 2b

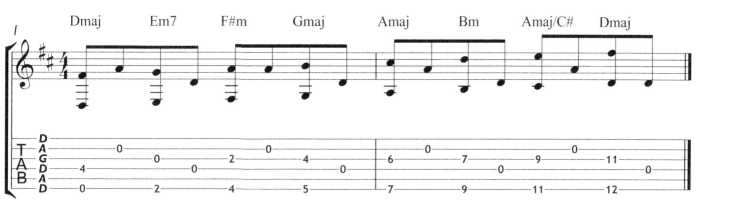

Using open strings in altered tunings lets you create chords and licks that can't be played in standard tuning. A beautiful and idiomatic way of doing this is to use *cascading scales*. This means using open strings in place of their fretted counterparts, and letting notes ring together to create a chiming, harp-like effect. Here's a cascading D Major scale in DADGAD tuning.

Example 2c

Cascading scales can be used to create melodies and licks, just like in this phrase where everything is drawn from the D Major scale. Remember to sustain the fretted notes against the open strings to create the ringing effect. Listen to the recording and you'll hear this in action.

Example 2d

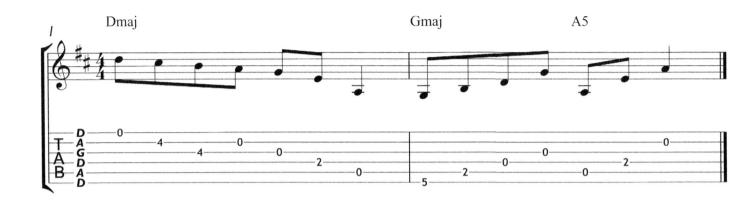

Let's explore some chords in the open position of DADGAD. Here the D Major scale is harmonized with scale tone chords in the open position.

Example 2e

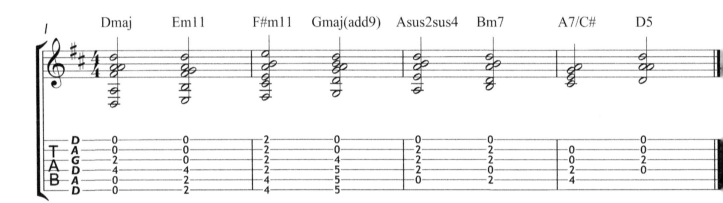

This chord progression is just a simple I ii vi V sequence in D Major (D – Em – Bm – A), but listen to how much richer it sounds played in DADGAD rather than standard tuning.

Example 2f

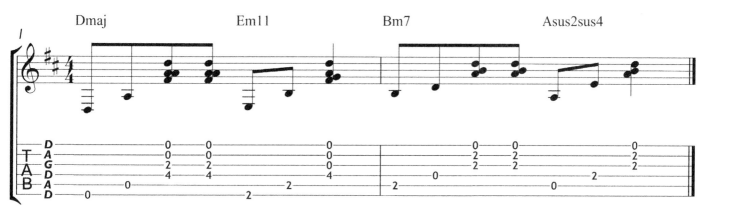

Finally, here's a musical example in DADGAD that starts with tenths in bar one before moving to a cascading D Major melody in bar two, followed by a pretty Em9 to Asus2sus4 in bars three and four.

Example 2g

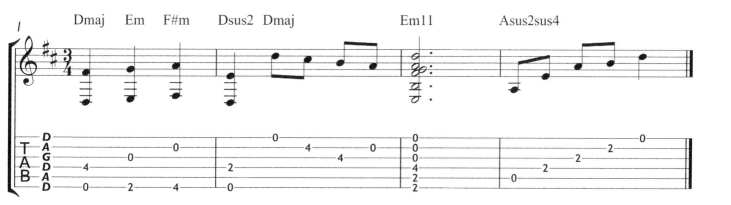

DADF#AD Tuning

Open D Major tuning (DADF#AD) is common in blues and slide guitar, but works really well in indie and folk guitar too. The open strings spell out a D major chord, so this tuning really pulls you into the key of D. However, many guitarists master one or two open tunings and simply use a capo allow them to play the same shapes in a different key higher up the neck.

We'll start by playing the D Major scale in tenths as we did earlier. All the notes on the low D string are the same as before, but the notes on the G string (now tuned to F#) have moved to accommodate the string being tuned a half step lower.

Example 2h

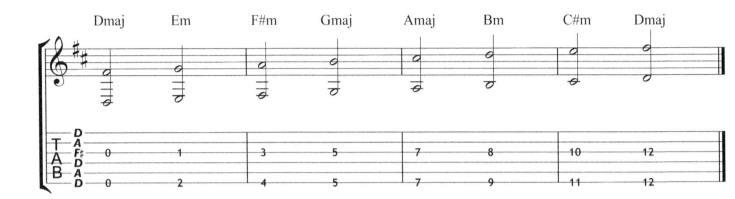

Again, the open strings do some of the work here and the results are similar to those in DADGAD. Look no further than Paul McCartney's *Blackbird* to hear tenths turned into iconic music.

Example 2i

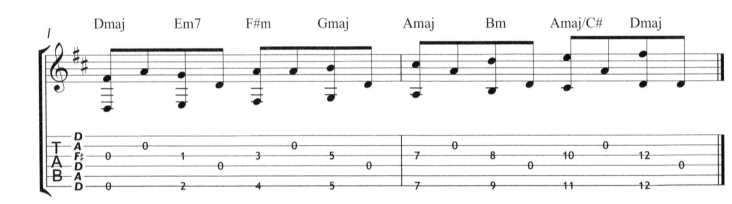

Next, is a cascading D Major scale in DADF#AD. From beat 3, the scale pattern is identical to the one in DADGAD.

Example 2j

Here's a cascading melody in DADF#AD. In bar one, it is melodic, while in bar two it's based around two arpeggiated chords: Bm (B, D, F#) and a second-inversion D major (A, D, F#).

Example 2k

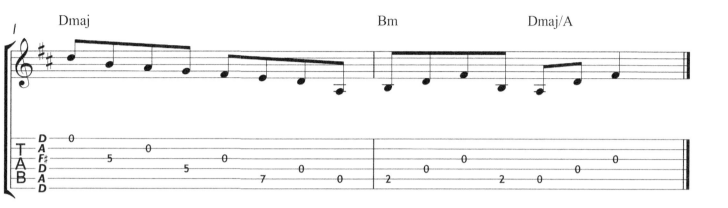

In this idea we harmonize the D Major scale with open position chords. With this approach, we have two options:

Harmonize up and down the neck using the sparse sound of tenths.

Play the full-sounding chords in the open position which make use of the open strings.

The texture and character of an altered tuning are revealed more clearly when we explore the open position chords.

Example 2l

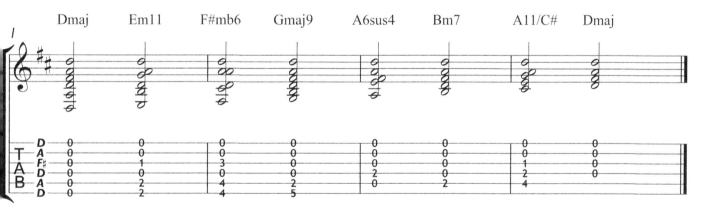

Now the chords are a simple I ii vi V progression (D – Em7 – Bm – A), but the open strings turn these chords into a richer sounding D major – Em7 – Bm7 – A6sus4.

You can play this with a pick or fingerpick, in which case, pick the low E and A strings with your thumb, then flick the strings down and up with your first finger.

Example 2m

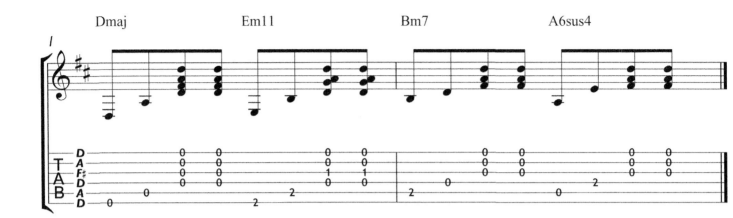

This example starts with an ascending idea in tenths followed by a cascading melody drawn from the D Major scale, and ends with two chords coloured by the open strings to create an Em11 and an A6sus4.

Example 2n

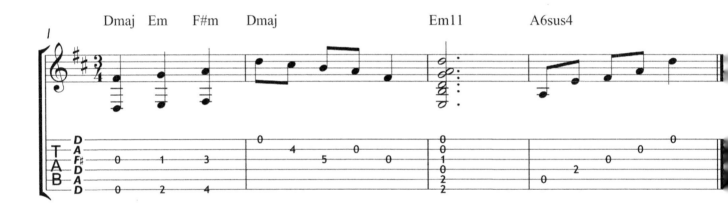

CGDGAD Tuning

Lower tunings can appear confusing at first, but this one is simply DADGAD with the low E and A strings tuned down an additional tone. Lower tunings like this have a deeper resonance and work well for solo singer/songwriters who require more depth, as they can create the illusion of playing with a bassist. However, they can be harder to use in a full band mix, where the low strings can introduce unwanted mud and get in the way of the actual bass or piano.

Again, here are tenth intervals in CGDGAD, but due to the tuning the tenths are easier to access on the low C and D strings. When you have learned them here, work them out on other string groupings. For example, start on the low C and D strings, then try moving to the low C and G strings where possible.

Example 2o

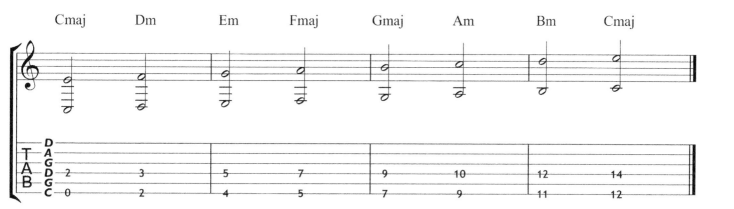

Here's a short study exploring tenths against open low A and G strings played as pedal tones. Remember, if an open string exists in the key of the tuning, you can use it as a pedal tone. Some open strings won't add much, but others will give real character. Experiment and have fun.

Example 2p

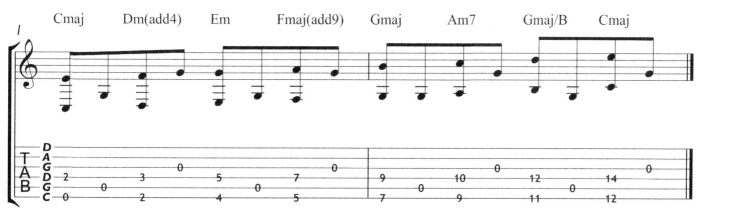

Try this cascading C Major scale. Notice that I don't begin on C, and instead choose to extend the range by starting the pattern from the 7th fret of the A string.

Example 2q

Here's a musical example using the cascading scale approach. Creating melodic ideas can just mean removing a few notes from the scale, so that it quickly starts to sound less like a scale pattern.

Example 2r

Lower tunings offer deep, evocative open position chord voicings, but these can sometimes present fingering challenges. The Dm11 in bar one is best played with your first finger fretted across the 2nd fret of the C and G strings, your second finger at the 3rd fret of the D string, and your third finger on the 3rd fret of the A string.

Example 2s

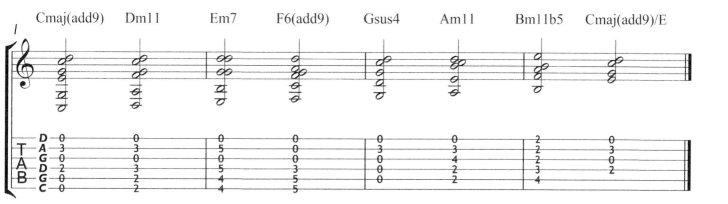

Open chords in low tunings take up a lot of harmonic space, so you may want to use them sparingly, even when playing solo! For the Am11 in bar two, your first finger barres the 2nd fret, your third finger is placed on the 4th fret, and your second finger is on the 3rd fret.

Example 2t

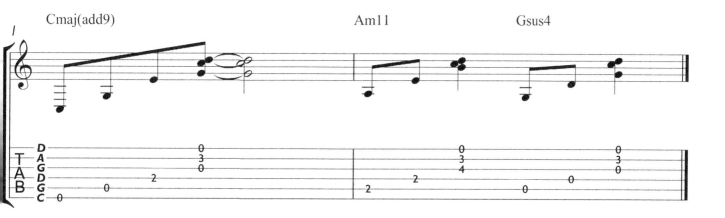

This example combines all the techniques you've studied in this section. It begins with tenths in bar one and moves to a cascading phrase in bar two, before finally exploring some lush-sounding chords in bars three and four.

Example 2u

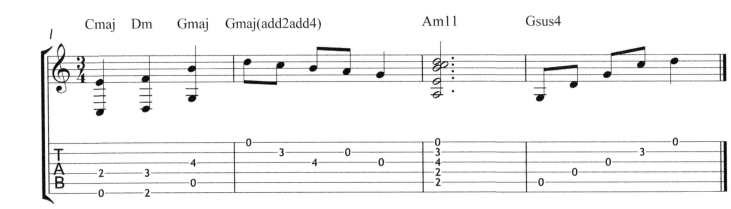

Chapter Three – The Americana Influence

At its heart, indie-folk contains a multitude of bands and artists who are all building their own musical worlds. These musicians share the same core techniques of fingerpicking and strumming, while bringing their own unique idiosyncrasies to the indie-folk universe. This encompasses everything from the complex altered tunings of Nick Drake and Ben Howard, to unconventional fingerpicking patterns, "rubber bridge" guitars, and unexpected twists to conventional harmony and chord progressions. Studying the artists in this chapter will introduce you to some new ideas and ways of hearing. No matter what kind of music you normally play, I guarantee you will discover some fresh approaches here.

Indie-folk is an extremely melodic genre, so we'll be exploring some rich chord voicings and altered tunings that create sounds which are almost impossible to make in standard tuning. Sometimes, these sounds are wistful and longing, other times they are full of tense dissonance. Some of these ideas are technically challenging with occasional idiosyncrasies, so listen carefully first, build the parts slowly, and then try to develop your own ideas from them.

Some of these artists use acoustic guitars exclusively (e.g., Nick Drake) while others move from acoustic to electric seamlessly. I use both acoustic and electric on the recordings, and while there are examples where one is more suitable than the other, there are many situations when either will do the job.

Many artists also use capos creatively – often high on the neck to create a brighter timbre. You can play all these examples without a capo, but where I've used one, I've indicated it above the example. While capos are traditionally used to make things easier for a vocalist's range, here they are used create richer tones or a brighter sound on guitar, where the low open strings could muddy things up.

We'll begin with some artists whose indie-folk sound carries a distinctly americana influence. These artists often play in standard tuning with occasional forays into Drop D.

The Avett Brothers

The Avett Brothers are one of the biggest bands in the indie-folk scene and are influenced by styles as diverse as bluegrass and country, to rock 'n' roll and folk. Scott and Seth Avett were initially influenced by grunge, but in their music there are hints of everyone from soul legend Sam Cooke and Hall and Oates, to country stars John Denver and Alan Jackson.

This is a typically Avett Brothers way of playing through an F – G – Am – G – C chord progression where subtle alterations to the chords create a wistful feel. The open G string in bar one adds a 9th to the F chord and the G in bar two becomes a Gsus4 with the addition of the C (1st fret, B string). Finally, in bar four the G is played with its 3rd (B) in the bass, which creates a smooth movement between the chords.

Example 3a

The bass runs on the C and G chords help to highlight their bluegrass/country influences and seem to be taken almost directly from Johnny Cash. The bass runs break up the progression and add another layer of texture to an otherwise standard chord sequence. All the bass notes are diatonic to the key G Major. The americana-style Csus2 chord in bar three is a nice, common alternative to C major.

Example 3b

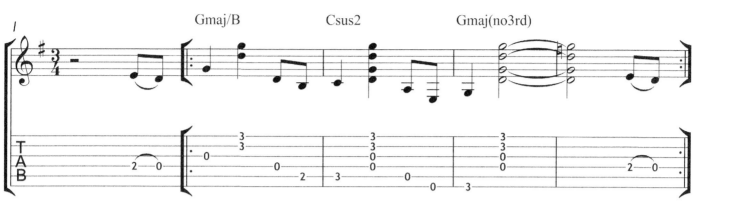

This C Major lick is strongly bluegrass in nature. The correct fingering will help get you up to speed, so use one finger per fret, starting with your first finger on the first fret. Once you can play this with hammer-ons, try picking every note for a more authentic bluegrass sound.

Example 3c

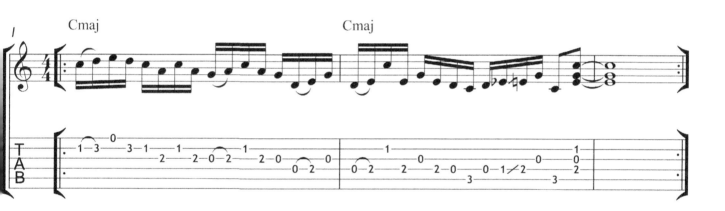

This example should be played with cross-picking (using a pick to pick every note). Your picking hand has a lot of work to do here, so master the chords first, so you can focus on the picking. Begin bar one with your second finger on the low E string and your third finger on the B string. Your first finger will take care of the notes at the 2nd fret of the G string.

Example 3d

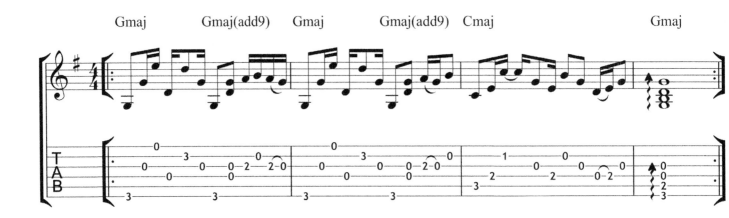

This example shows some interesting ways of colouring a D – A – D – G progression in Drop D. In bar one, the open strings create different textures as we move from a D6(sus2sus4) to a Dadd4, both of which are more interesting than a basic D major chord. The Dadd4 shape in bar three is one of the most common in indie-folk and americana, and a great substitute for D major in Drop D tuning.

Example 3e

CAPO FRET 5

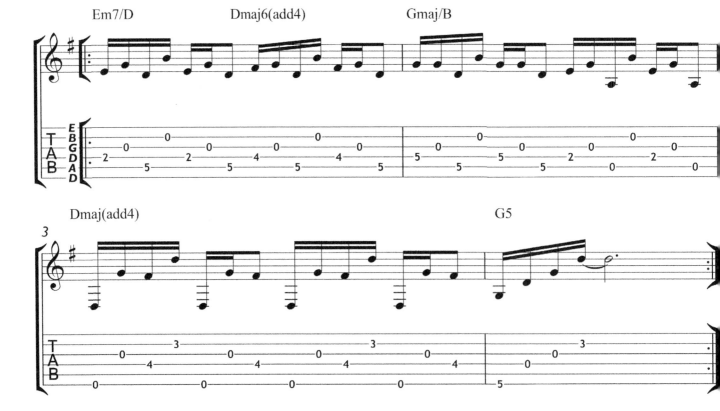

Gregory Alan Isakov

South African by birth but resident in the USA since 1986, Gregory Alan Isakov is an independent musician in the truest sense, self-releasing his albums via his own Suitcase Town Music label. Falling somewhere between indie-folk and americana, he has drawn influence from Bluesman Kelly Joe Phelps, Leonard Cohen, and fellow indie-folk act Iron and Wine. In this section we will explore some of his stylistic approaches.

The more you explore fingerstyle playing, the more you will start to recognise when common patterns are useful, and when you should move away from traditional picking hand approaches. In this example, use your picking hand thumb on the low E string, your second finger on the open D, your first finger on the A string, and your third finger on the open G string.

Example 3f

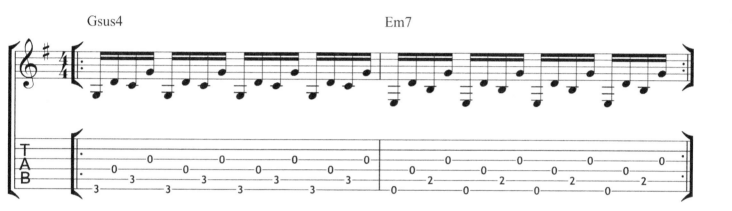

You'll also see familiar chord embellishments emerging. The most challenging embellishment here is the stretch in bar four to form the Csus2 chord. Start with your third finger on the A string and your first finger on the B string. On beat 4, keep the first finger in place and add your fourth finger at the 4th, followed by your second finger on the 2nd fret.

Example 3g

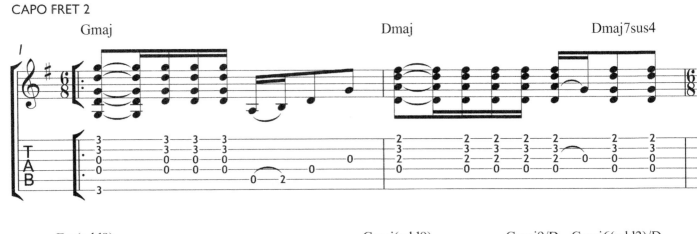

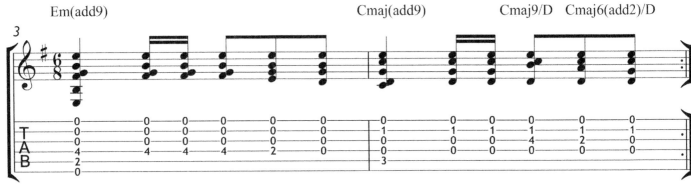

Syncopation (playing notes off the beat) is one of the most challenging areas of folk fingerpicking. Begin by learning to focus just on your thumb picking pattern to begin with. When you are confident, learn the top line separately. When you can hum one rhythm while playing the other, try putting them together.

Example 3h

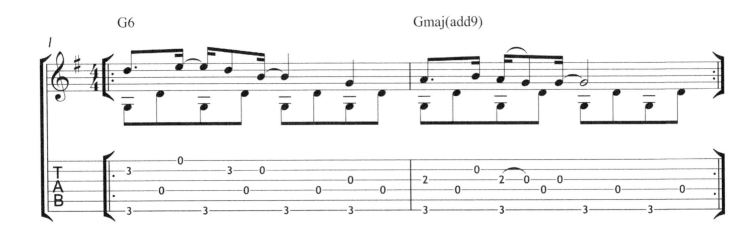

Embellished chords are at the core of this next idea. Before playing examples like this, see if there are common tones that exist between the chords as they are a regular feature of indie-folk guitar. In this case, use your first finger to hold the C note on the B string throughout, and your third and second fingers for the notes on the 3rd and 2nd frets.

Example 3i

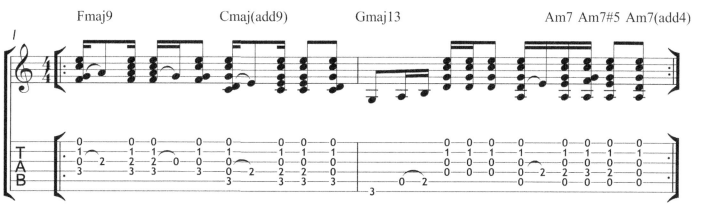

This chord sequence includes two common tones. Use your first and fourth fingers here, and use your second finger for 2nd fret notes and your third for those on the 3rd fret.

Example 3j

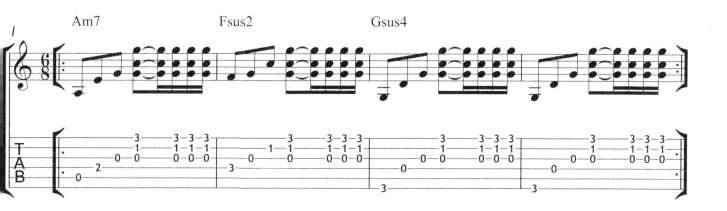

First Aid Kit

Swedish folk duo, Johanna and Klara Soderberg found fame with their release of a Fleet Foxes cover on YouTube in 2008. Guitarist Klara was influenced by classic country from Johnny Cash, Bob Dylan, The Carter Family, and more. You can hear this in her guitar style, which draws more from the traditional country/folk sound than those players who veer towards modern altered tunings. As such, she is a great study for any player new to this genre, or for fingerpicking in general.

With their use of 1960's inspired open chords and fingerpicking patterns, First Aid Kit are a great blend of traditional folk styles. This example can be strummed with a pick, but if you prefer fingerstyle, brush the strings with the nail of your first finger. The chords are played as full, then broken chords, which creates a cool, almost piano-like contrast between the higher and lower registers.

Example 3k

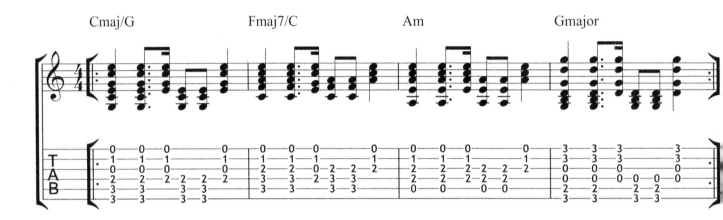

We start with a folk picking pattern on an E minor chord, which creates a 1960's-style retro vibe. The tenth intervals in bar two sound thinner and contrast with the busy picking in bar one.

Example 3l

This example looks complex, but it's all played within chord shapes. As you play the pull-offs in the chord shapes, it's important to keep the other fingers fretted. For example, for the F chord in bar one, keep your third finger down on the 3rd fret and your first finger at the 1st fret, while your second finger performs the pull-off on the G string. Repeat this for the C major chord, with your third and second fingers a string higher.

Example 3m

There are more classic folk fingerpicking approaches on an A major chord here. Simple parts like this can be a great study in dynamics, so explore how you can vary the volume on the picking hand fingers by either digging in or easing back. You can get more mileage out of this exercise by palm muting the A and D strings, while allowing the remaining strings to ring.

Example 3n

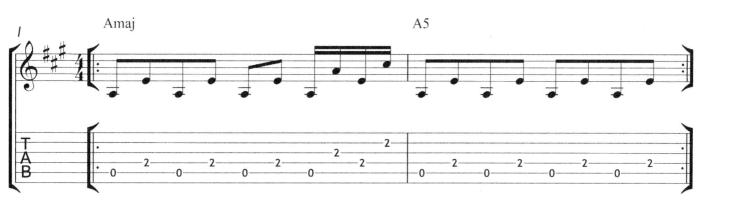

You can play this brisk waltz with a pick or fingers. The chords are straightforward, but the tempo places more demands on the picking hand. Aside from the pace, ensure your timing remains consistent and pay particular attention to the contrasting feel as the bars alternate from busy to sparse.

Example 3o

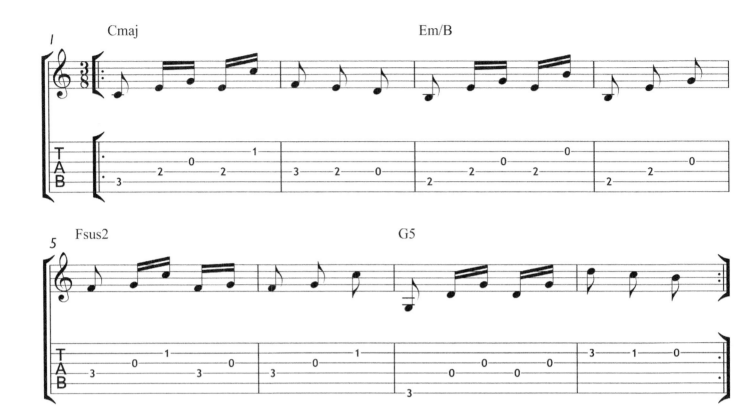

The Civil Wars

Grammy award winning duo Joy Williams (piano/vocals) and John Paul White (guitar/vocals) only released two albums as The Civil Wars, but quicky found success through their incredible vocal harmonies and sublime songwriting. White is a great example of how traditional folk and americana guitar has been updated for a more modern sound, and the tone of his 1957 Martin 000-18 acoustic is about as folk/americana as it gets! A melodic fingerpicker and strummer, his stunning guitar parts go beyond simple accompaniment.

Texture and colour are at the heart of John Paul White's guitar part writing, and he'll often inject subtle tension into chords. This C – Em progression gets a tense twist by his use of a Cmaj7#11 chord in place of a straight C major. The #11 comes from the F# in the chord and this note is on the 4th fret of the D string.

Example 3p

CAPO FRET 7

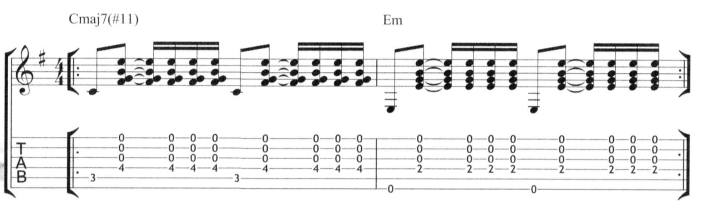

White regularly replaces simple chords with something more evocative. In this case, he plays an Em9 voicing in place of a standard E minor chord. The minor 9th is the F# at the 4th fret of the D string. When playing the embellishment on beat 1, keep your second finger on the 3rd fret of the B string, so the notes on the G string ring against it.

Example 3q

CAPO FRET 7

White also explores higher register chords and, in this example, he outlines a D major triad (D, F#, A) in bar one and uses the open E string to turn the chord into a more colourful Dadd9. In bar two he turns this into a Dmaj9 simply by lowering the note on the G string a semitone from D to C#, and uses the open E string again to provide the 9th of the chord.

Example 3r

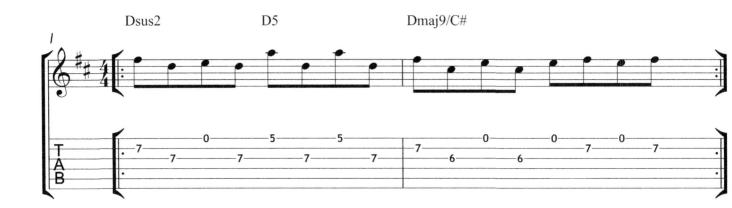

White's sparse approach to chords is essential when he's playing against a full sounding piano or band mix. In this example, everything is achieved on just the A, B and E strings, with the only movement coming from a descending bassline on the A string. This is a great writing tool and the moving bass notes dictate the overall sound of the chords.

Example 3s

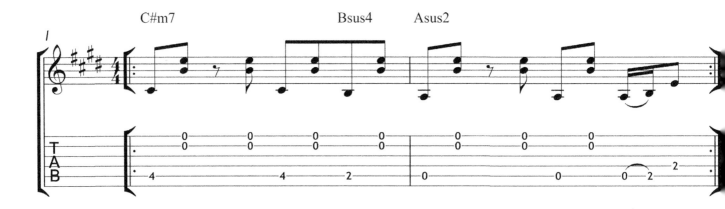

In this example, a Bb major to D minor chord progression is given some tension. In bar one, White uses a basic Bb major triad on the D, G and B strings, and the open E string adds a #11, which yields a tense sounding Bbmaj7#11. In bar two he uses the open E string to create a lush Dm(add9) and replaces this with the B (the 7th fret on the E string) for a dissonant Dm6.

Example 3t

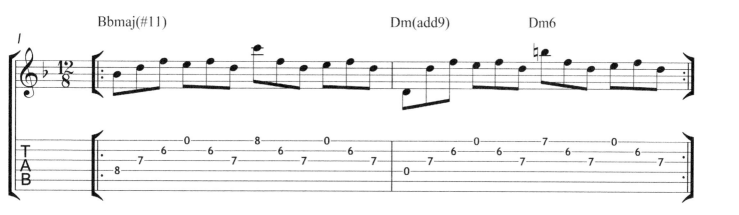

Milk Carton Kids

The American indie-folk duo Milk Carton Kids comprises guitarists and singers Kenneth Pattengale and Joey Ryan. The duo formed in 2011 and found success with a Grammy nomination for their 2013 album *The Ash and Clay*. They are a great study for acoustic players with Pattengale's melodic lead lines soaring over Ryan's traditional folk fingerpicking. Their lead and accompaniment parts come together perfectly.

In our first example, we see how Joey Ryan's fingerpicking is influenced by Bob Dylan and Paul Simon, where a common fingerpicking pattern of an 1/8th note rhythm on beat 1 is followed by a busier 1/16th note pattern on beat 2.

Bar two features the "folk F" chord. Hook your thumb over the 1st fret of the E string, use your third finger on the D string, and your first finger on the 1st fret of the B string.

Example 3u

Kenneth Pattengale often improvises detailed lines over Ryan's chords and here he outlines the chords and adds some extensions. In bar one we play a Cadd9 chord and an Fmaj7 in bar two. The rhythms are the same as before.

Example 3v

Varying fingerpicking rhythms is a rich writing tool that can give simple parts some interesting movements. Here, Ryan takes the simple chord progression of Bm – G major – Em – A major, and adds urgency to the rhythms by playing a dotted 1/8th to 1/16th pattern on beat 2, followed by 1/4 notes on beats 3 and 4 to slow things down again.

Example 3w

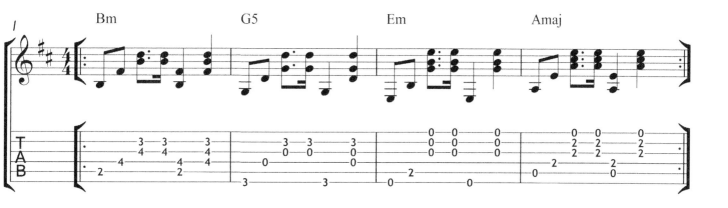

The consistent, sparse rhythm of the previous example gives Pattengale plenty of space to play busier lines. He uses the G Major scale to mirror the chords and takes advantage of the open G string as a pedal tone in bar one. In bar four he outlines the A major chord with an A major triad line high on the neck. Remember to use a capo at the 7th fret for this one!

Example 3x

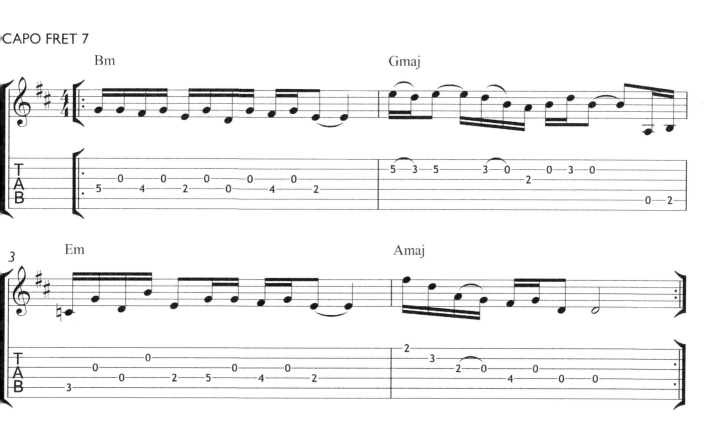

Chapter Four – The Art Folk Sound

In this chapter we'll explore artists who draw more from traditional folk to create their own versions of modern indie-folk. As with the previous chapter, these artists predominantly use standard tuning.

Damien Rice

Irish singer-songwriter Damien Rice found mainstream success with his 2002 debut album *O,* which had three UK top 30 singles.

Rice is one of the most significant artists in the indie-folk scene and his musical DNA can be traced down to artists like Mumford and Sons and Ben Howard. Even Ed Sheeran cites him as an influence. Rice himself was inspired by classic rock/folk artists such as John Lennon and Paul Simon.

We'll begin this section with a look at some of his stylistic traits.

Indie-folk guitarists commonly embellish open chords like the ones below with hammer-ons and pull-offs. Start this example with an open position C major chord, release your second finger to the open D string, then hammer back on to the 2nd fret.

In bar two, a G major is modified to become a Gadd4 using a common tone (C) that links both chords.

Example 4a

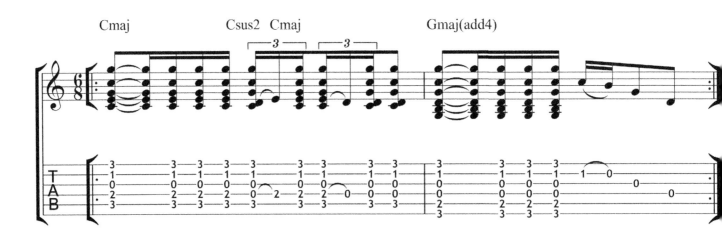

This idea places a moving melody against the open G string, which serves as a pedal tone to fill out the texture. If you are fingerpicking, try brushing down the D and G strings together with the nail of your first finger. In bar two, let the 3rd fret ring as you play the melody on the B string.

Example 4b

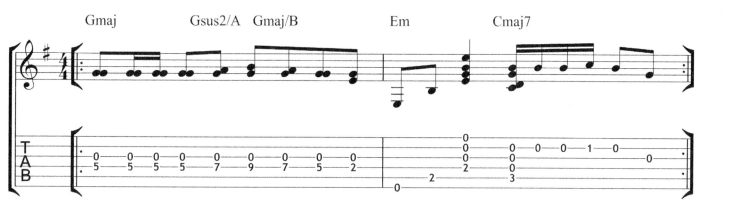

There are various ways you could pick this example, but I suggest using your picking hand thumb on the E string followed by your first finger on the A string. Then use your second finger for the D, and your third for the G string. Often, *rolling* down the strings with these fingers is easier than playing them with your thumb.

Example 4c

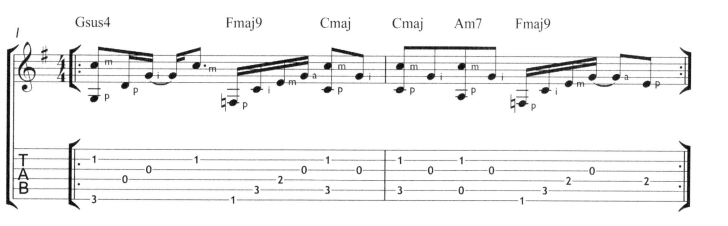

A simple C major – D major – G major progression is enriched with more colourful chords in this example. C major is replaced by a Cadd9. On beat 3 we play Dadd11 with the 3rd of the chord (F#) in the bass, which leads smoothly to G Major in the next bar.

Example 4d

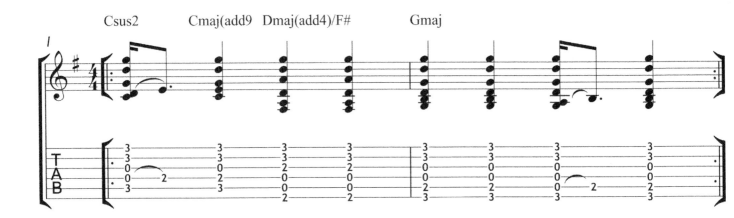

Low register chords can sound full, yet avoid any muddiness, if you add open strings against the low fretted notes. The ringing open strings add both clarity and colour. This may not always work in a busy band setting, but in small ensembles or solo performances it creates a sound that is integral to indie-folk part writing.

Example 4e

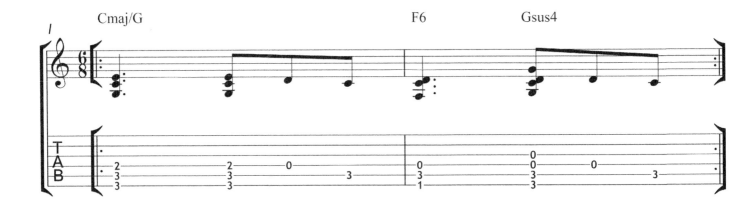

Fleet Foxes

Fleet Foxes define the indie-folk sound with tight vocal harmonies and folk-tinged acoustic guitar parts. They formed in 2006 and take influence from classic songwriters like Bob Dylan and Neil Young, as well as folk legend Roy Harper. However, it is perhaps the Crosby, Stills and Nash influence which is most prominent in their music. Throughout their catalogue, guitarists Robin Pecknold and Christian Wargo create interwoven parts that support the group's stunning vocal harmonies.

We'll begin with this challenging, yet beautiful rolling pattern. Use your third finger at the 3rd fret of the E string, your fourth finger on the 4th fret of the D string, and first finger on the G string, 2nd fret. Remember to keep the third finger in place throughout, and use my suggested picking pattern to keep things flowing smoothly.

Example 4f

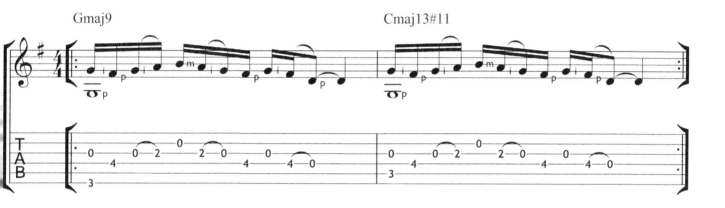

This classical-sounding idea shows how tenth intervals can be used to create strong yet simple harmonic parts. In bar two, hook your fretting hand thumb over the neck to play the 2nd fret of the E string. Use your second finger on the 2nd fret of the G string, and your third finger on the B string.

Example 4g

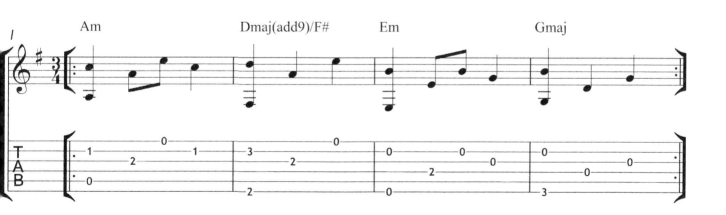

The next example is an idiomatic *reverse roll*. For the G chord, place your second finger on the 3rd fret of the low E string, and use your fourth finger to add the note at the 4th fret of the D string. Descend to the 3rd fret with your third finger.

The Cmaj13 chord can be played with your second first fingers.

Example 4h

This example is a workout for the picking hand as your thumb outlines a repeating 1/8th note bassline with a syncopated melody played on top. For the melody, pick beat 1 with your first finger on the D string then your second finger on the open G. Repeat this pattern for the "&" of beat 1 and use your second finger for all notes on the B string.

Example 4i

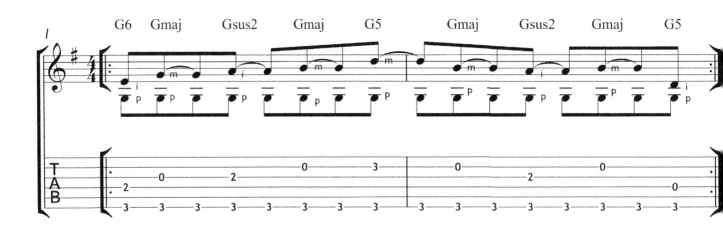

In this example, high register major and minor triads are used in the part writing.

You could use a pick, but I suggest fingerpicking this due to the tempo. Use your first, second and third fingers to pick the G, B and E strings.

Example 4j

Iron And Wine

Recording under the stage name Iron and Wine, Sam Beam is an American indie-folk artist from South Carolina. The first Iron and Wine album was released on the iconic indie label Sub Pop in 2002, and received comparisons to Nick Drake, Simon and Garfunkel, Elliott Smith and John Fahey. Beam's use of acoustic guitar, slide guitar, and banjo makes him another artist who successfully blurs the boundaries between indie-folk and americana.

Playing the A fretted, rather than as an open string, keeps the sound of this first example a little tighter. Try playing bar one with your second finger on the low E string, your first finger on the 4th fret, and your third finger on the 6th fret. If that feels uncomfortable, release your second finger from the low E and play the open A string instead.

Example 4k

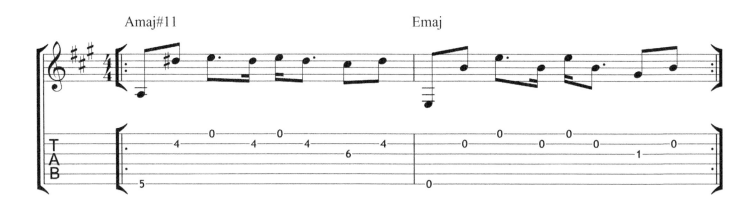

This is another example where simple chords (in this case power chords) come to life when played against open strings. If you're fingerpicking, use the picking hand thumb for the A and D strings, your first finger for the G string, and your second finger for the B string. Alternatively, use your thumb for the A string, your first finger for the D string, your second finger on the G string, and your third finger for the B string.

Example 4l

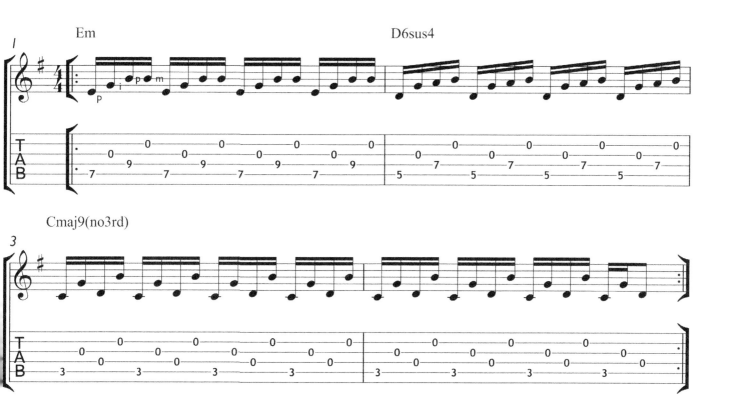

The rich sound of unisons (the same pitched played in two places at the same time) is a common feature in folk and indie-folk. You'll see this here in bars three and four, where the D note appears on the 5th fret of the A string and the open D string. Fret this chord with your fourth finger on the A string and your first finger on the G string. Ensure your fourth finger doesn't accidentally mute the open A.

Example 4m

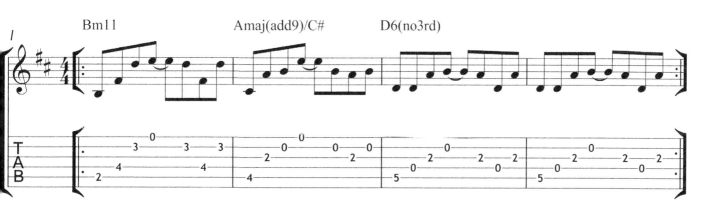

You can play this idea with a pick or fingerstyle. If you're using your fingers, play beat 1 with a thumb-thumb-first finger pattern, then from beat 2 use thumb-thumb-first-second finger.

Example 4n

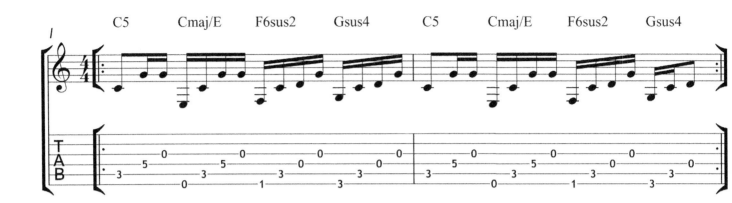

Drop D tuning can be used when you want to easily access a IV or V chord. Here, we're in the key of A, so the low open D string brings a colourful D6/9sus4 chord.

Example 4o

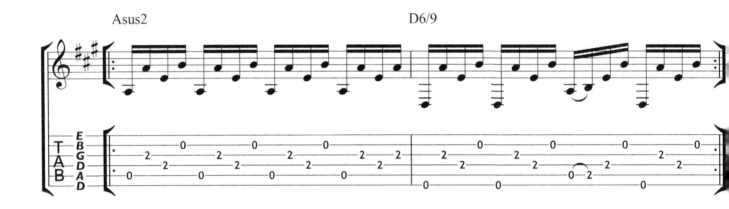

The Decemberists

Although they have a heavier sound that leans more towards indie rock, you'll find some great indie-folk style playing on both acoustic and electric from guitarists Colin Meloy and Chris Funk in The Decemberists. Open string chord voicings feature prominently in their sound and bring something new to standard chord progressions.

Using moveable shapes with open strings is a fantastic tool when writing indie-folk parts. This Bm – G major – D major chord progression is rejuvenated by playing it with just one shape that moves around the neck. Open strings add different textures, so listen to how the character of the open D and E strings affects the chords as you move.

Example 4p

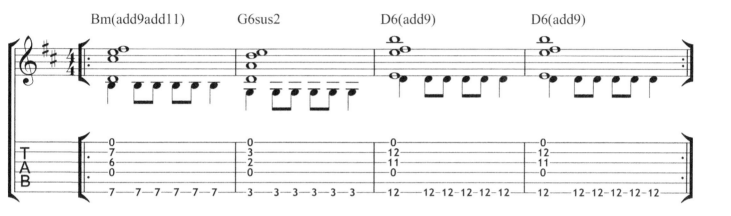

The next two examples sit together. The first is a common chord progression that gains character as the chords are divided into a low/high strumming approach, and an alternating sparse/busy rhythmic pattern.

You don't need to be 100% accurate when breaking up chords like this, just aim for a general low to high string contrast.

Example 4q

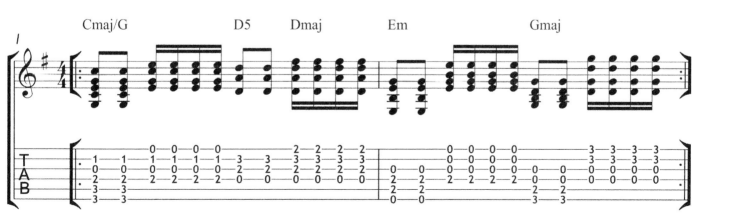

This G Major melody line sits on top of the previous example. The melody sounds cohesive as it generally starts from the root of a chord tone of the underlying chord.

Example 4r

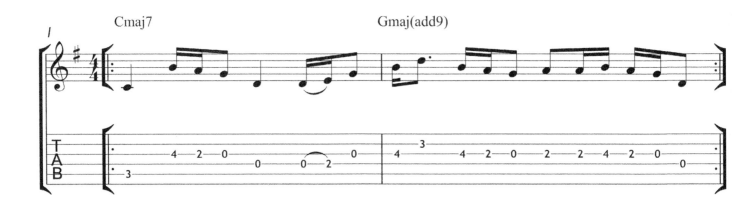

This example shows you a wonderful way to gain mileage out of the I chord. The notes on the E and A strings remain static, while movement on the D string takes you from a Gmaj7 to a G6 and finally a G major. In bar one, use your second finger on the E string, your first finger on the A string, and your fourth finger on the D string. In bar two, your first finger barres the A and D strings at the 2nd fret.

Example 4s

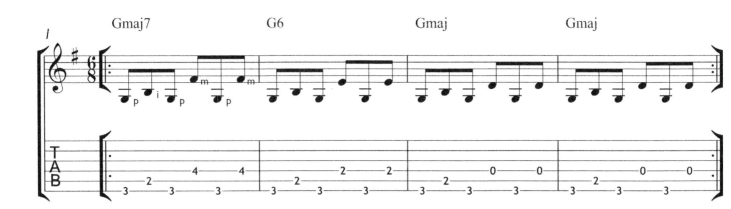

Here's another example of how open strings transform a common progression. In bar one, the Cmaj7 chord is given weight with the open G, B and E strings, which add the 5th, 7th and 3rd of the chord. In bar two, an Em7 is thickened by adding the open E and B strings to the voicing.

Example 4t

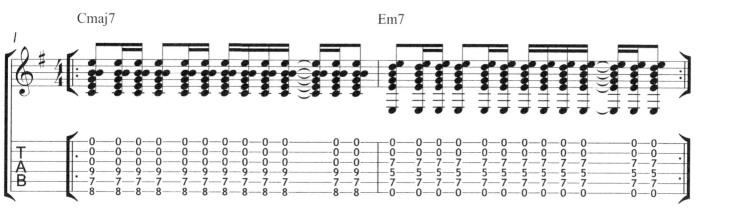

The Lumineers

Often labelled as alternative folk, The Lumineers draw influence from Bob Dylan, Leonard Cohen, Guns N' Roses and Tom Petty, amongst others. As with The Avett Brothers, they have found huge success without deviating from their alt-folk origins and have written songs for Hollywood movies like The Hunger Games. By their own admission they write "simple songs" but the instrumentation and textural, folk-inspired guitar parts contribute hugely to their unique sound.

Many guitarists avoid low F barre chords as much as possible, and that's fine because better sounding alternatives often exist. The Fmaj7 shape allows you to create movement within the chord by moving from the 2nd fret to the open G string.

Example 4u

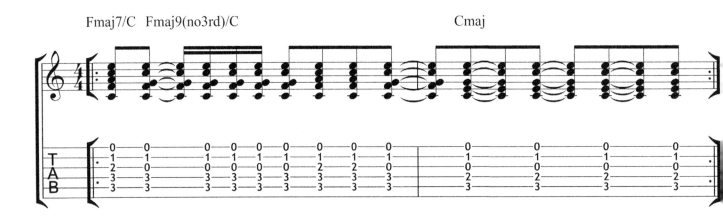

This decorated C – F – G chord progression is outlined on just the D, G and B strings.

It begins with a first inversion C major triad, moves to an F6/9, and is followed by a G6. Playing chords like this offers interesting phrasing options, so notice how your third finger can slide from the 3rd to the 5th fret of the D string to move from F to the G.

Example 4v

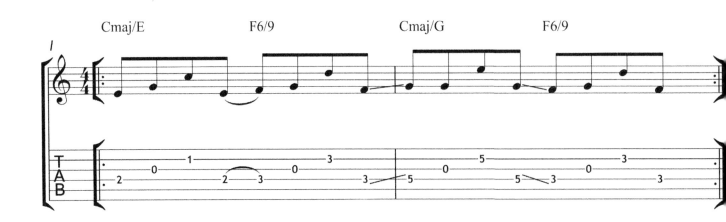

The next sound is essentially A major, but by moving notes on the E string we can create different tonalities that provide an interesting alternative to just strumming a single chord. Try playing this with hybrid picking, where the pick plays the G string while the middle finger plays the high E string.

Example 4w

This Am – C – F sequence is given more colour by substituting open strings for the fretted notes you'd normally play. The Fmaj9 chord in bar two is an indie-folk favourite. To play it, hook your thumb over the neck to fret the E string, then use your third and fourth fingers on the A and D strings respectively, and your first finger on the B string.

Example 4x

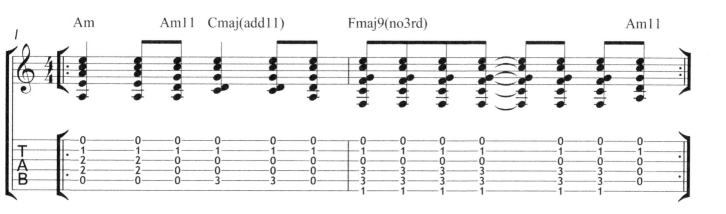

Here's a traditional folk-style approach to breaking up a C major chord and it's all in the movement low down in the chord. Keep your first finger on the 1st fret of the B string throughout as the other notes move around it, with your third finger taking care of anything at the 3rd fret, and your second finger reserved for the notes at the 2nd fret.

Example 4y

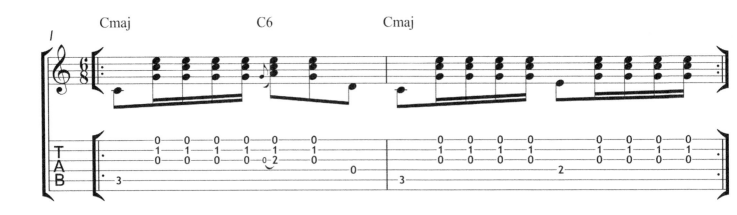

Chapter Five – Altered Tunings Part One

In this chapter you'll study the styles and approaches of artists who draw from the folk genre along with indie, world, rock and more. You'll also discover how these artists incorporate altered tunings into their writing alongside standard tuning.

Bombay Bicycle Club

Bombay Bicycle Club formed in 2005 while its members were still at school and their sound continues to evolve, drawing influence from the folk world via John Martyn and Nick Drake. Guitarist Jamie Macoll has an incredible musical heritage himself, being the grandson of folk royalty Ewan Macoll, and the nephew of Kirsty Macoll. The band's eclectic sound also takes influence from The Smiths and indie rock giants Pavement, but the following ideas explore Macoll's more folk-based style.

Indie-folk guitarists often eschew basic major and minor chords for more colourful variants, so let's start with this rich-sounding Em9 to Gmaj13 idea. In bar two, keep your second and third fingers in place while playing the hammer-on on the A string. For the Gmaj13 (Em9/B) in bar two, use your second finger on the E string, your fourth finger on the D string, your first finger on the G string, and your third finger on the B string.

Example 5a

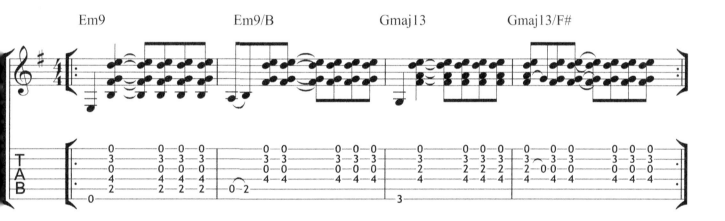

Using pull-offs within shapes is a quick way to embellish simple chords. In bar two, use your first finger on the D string and your second finger on the G string. Use the third finger for the E string pull-off, and your fourth finger on the 3rd fret of the B string, followed by your third finger at the 2nd fret.

Example 5b

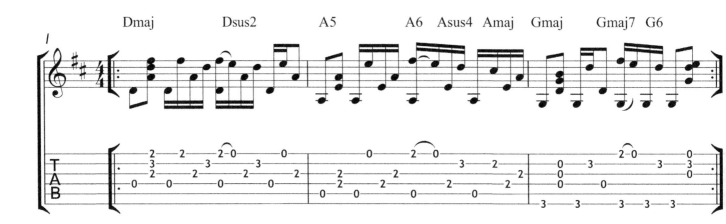

Here's another example of chord enrichment. The basic progression is Em – C – G, but is played as Em9, Cmaj9 and G, using open strings. To play the C chords in bar two, use your second finger on the E string and your third finger on the B string, to allow smooth movement down to the open G major.

Example 5c

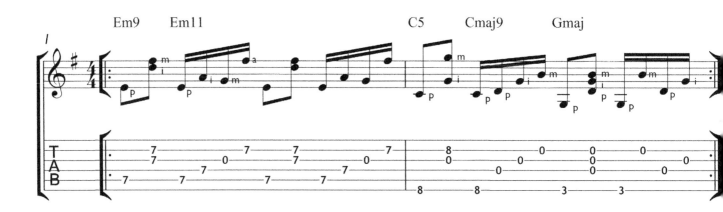

This example explores the lower register played against the open D and G strings. The E and A strings played together can sound muddy, but adding open strings after each chord adds colour and clarity, especially on the Cadd9 and Am11 chords, and makes this simple progression comes to life.

Keep the open strings ringing throughout for clarity.

Example 5d

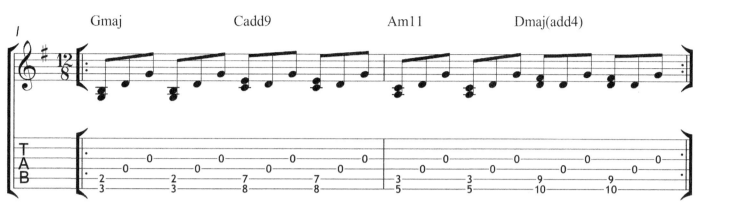

The next example is in open D Major tuning (DADF#AD) and shows how much work an open tuning can do for you. This example is made up of mostly open strings with a handful of fretted notes, yet still sounds incredibly melodic.

However, to avoid "accidents" when creating parts like this, make sure you know where the root note of each chord is. For example, in bar two, we easily move to an E minor chord by starting at the 2nd fret of the low D string.

Example 5e

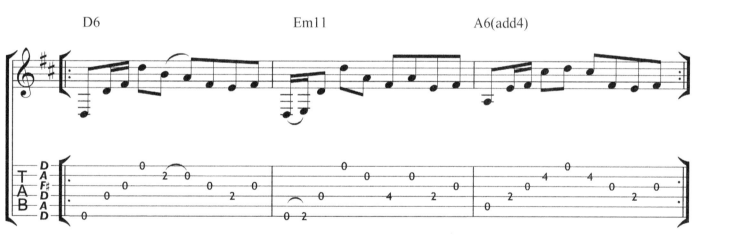

Kristin Hersh

Kristin Hersh came to prominence with the rock band Throwing Muses. However, as a solo artist she has a sparser indie/folk sound that explores more angular, dissonant tones. Starting her solo career in 1994, she became a pioneer of indie-folk, and releases her own music as an independent musician. Her influences are wide ranging and include elements from bands as diverse as The Carter Family, The Clash, and Talking Heads.

Hersh often uses "parallel movement" in her chordal approach, which is just a fancy way of saying "moves the same chord shape up and down the neck". Writing like this is easier when several open string notes belong to the key, like E, A, D, G and C.

In this example, keep the high E string ringing by using your first finger on the D string, second finger on the G string, and third on the B string.

Example 5f

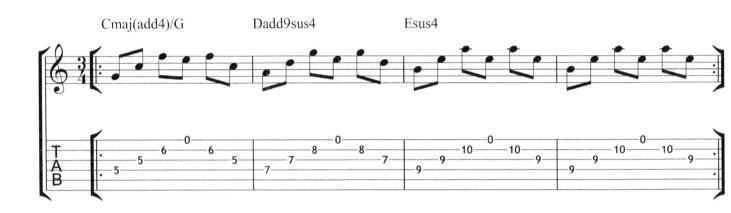

Here's another example of moving a shape up and down the neck, and where open strings give each chord more character. Fingerpick this with your thumb playing the A and D strings, and your first, second and third fingers sounding the G, B and E strings respectively.

Example 5g

In this example, we move a basic power chord shape around the neck with the open G string adding character to each chord. This can be played with a pick, or be fingerpicked with your thumb on the low E string, followed by your first, second and third fingers plucking the A, D and E strings.

Example 5h

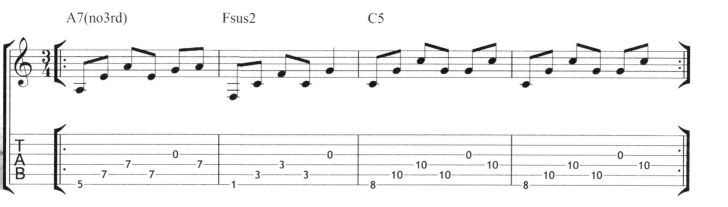

Next, the open D string roots this idea in key of D and gives the simple root + fifth power chords more character. If fingerpicking, use your thumb to strike the low E and A strings together, followed by your first finger on the open D string.

When writing like this, it's useful to consider what interval the open string will add to each chord. Is it a 9th, an 11th, a 7th, or simply doubling up a note that's already in the chord?

Example 5i

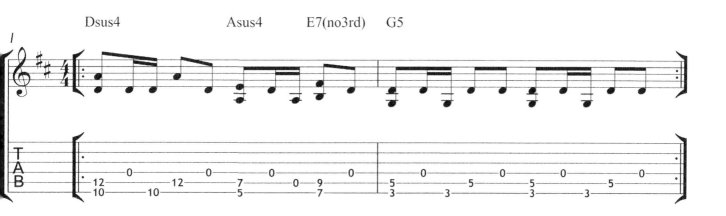

This riff-based example demonstrates again how Hersh uses open strings for colour and can be played with pick or fingers. If fingerpicking, use your thumb for the E and A strings in bars one and two, then your first finger for the D string. Bars three and four use a more common pattern of thumb for the A and D strings, first finger for the G string, and second finger for the B string.

Example 5j

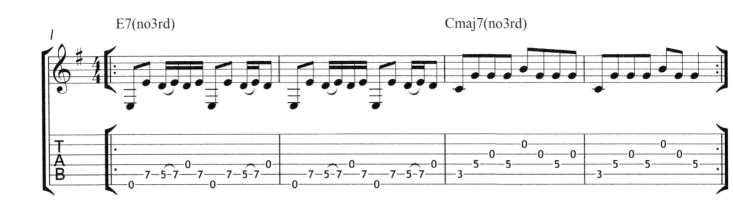

Laura Marling

British singer-songwriter Laura Marling began her music career when she moved to London aged 16. She immersed herself in the nu-folk movement and worked with Noah and The Whale and Mumford and Sons before developing her solo career. Her main influences are Bob Dylan and Elliott Smith, and Smith's tense, dissonant chordal approach can often be heard in her playing.

This example starts off by weaving between A minor and E major chords, but Marling's voicings add some sophistication here. This is a great lesson in how chord inversions can be used to create descending basslines. Check out the smooth bass movement from A to E7 in bar one using a first inversion E7 chord, which has the third (G#) in the bass.

Example 5k

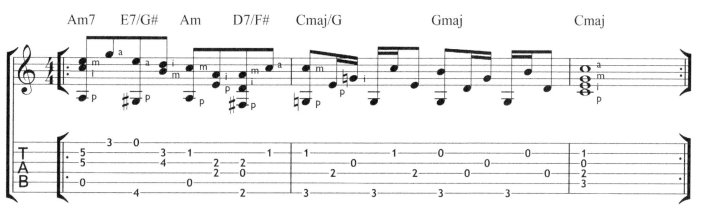

Marling's chords are full of character, and she often creates space by avoiding playing full shapes, as with the sparse F#7 on beat 2. Many players would hold down a barre shape for this, but she elects to pick notes on just the A, G and E strings for a more spacious texture.

Example 5l

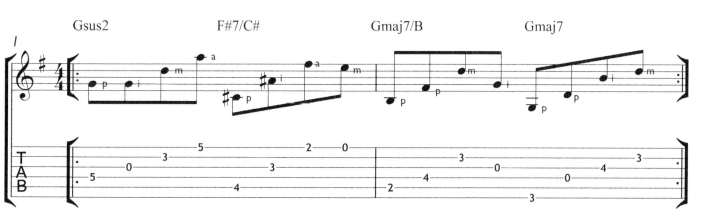

This movement from G major to C major is a classic folk phrase borrowed from Bob Dylan and Paul Simon. Use your third finger at the 3rd fret and hammer on to the D and B strings with your second and first fingers. The D6/F# chord in bar two is another classic folk voicing with the third (F#) in the bass of the chord.

Example 5m

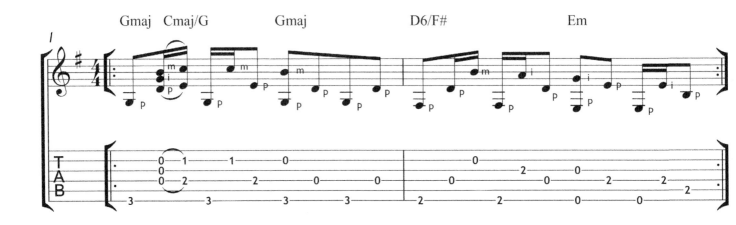

Let's explore DADGAD tuning in this example, which creates some rich voicings without thirds.

The second bar features syncopations between the bassline and the melody on the top strings. Learn these parts independently to begin with. The picking hand thumb takes care of the bass notes and your first and second fingers are used to pluck the B and E strings.

Example 5n

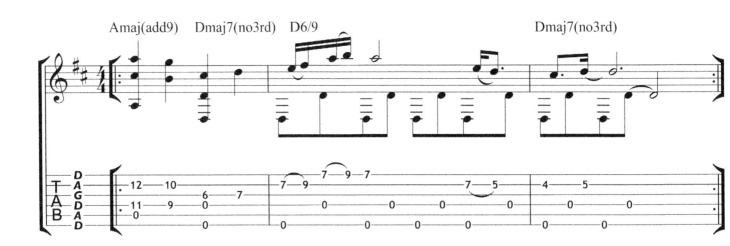

Marling often uses open D Minor tuning (DADFAD), a close cousin of DADGAD but with an entirely different sound. Whereas DADGAD is a modal tuning that doesn't have a major or minor tonality, DADFAD spells out a D minor chord, and so pulls you towards minor key writing.

Marling frequently uses this tuning to conjure up Bach-like chordal passages such as this one.

Example 5o

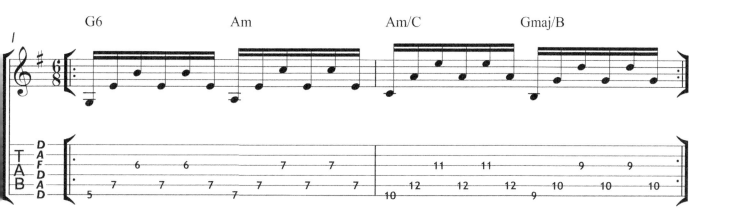

Mumford And Sons

Some acts like Mumford and Sons manage to transcend genre boundaries and enter the mainstream. Perhaps best classified as folk-rock, they formed in 2007 and centre around Marcus Mumford's guitar and vocals, and Winston Marshall's banjo. Mumford's driving acoustic guitar parts often feature altered tunings, but he generally avoids the dissonance of other indie-folk artists like Elliott Smith and Laura Marling. The band often play energetically at high tempos and Mumford's strumming hand is a great study in attack and stamina.

Marcus Mumford frequently uses tenth intervals and adds a pedal tone in between the two strings. In this C Major example, the open G string is played between the tenths on the A and B strings. This allows us to outline chords all over the neck without getting stuck in the open position.

Example 5p

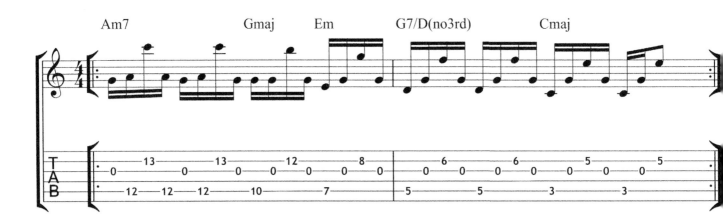

Now an open B string pedal is played between sixth intervals on the G and E strings. Fingerpick this with your thumb on the G string, your second finger on the B string, and your first finger on the E string. You can also hybrid pick, so that the pick plays the G and B strings and your first finger strikes the E string.

Example 5q

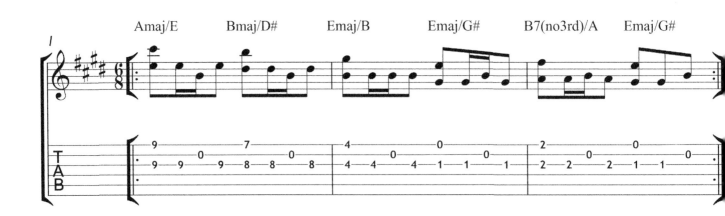

Next, let's move to Mumford's favoured open D Major tuning (DADF#AD). We can, however, keep the "tenths plus pedal tone" approach. This time tenths are played on the E and G strings and the pedal is the open D string. Taking this approach, this simple chord sequence sounds incredibly rich, and we also get to add descending/ascending movement.

Example 5r

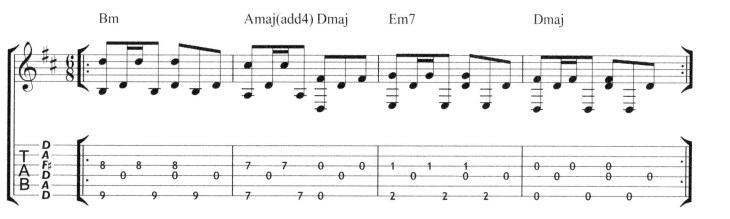

A big advantage of open tunings is that you can achieve more with fewer fingers, as the open strings do so much work! Marcus Mumford would use a pick for this example. On beat 3 of bar one, check out how easy it is to move to G major, which requires just two fingers from the fretting hand.

Example 5s

CAPO FRET 4

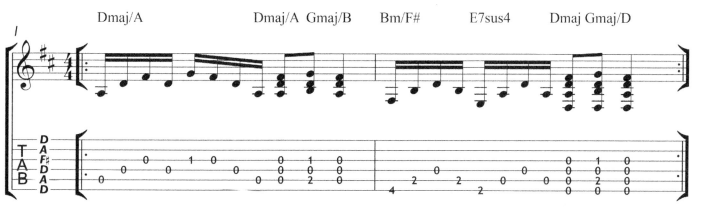

Mumford's powerful rhythmic style is in evidence here, and again the tuning takes care of much of the work. Bar one features a simple, one-fingered Bm7 chord and Mumford often builds parts from these simple voicings with a heavy right-hand attack for a huge sound.

Palm mute the open strings and the sound explodes! Bar two features a lovely Gadd9 to D major progression, again simplified by the tuning.

Example 5t

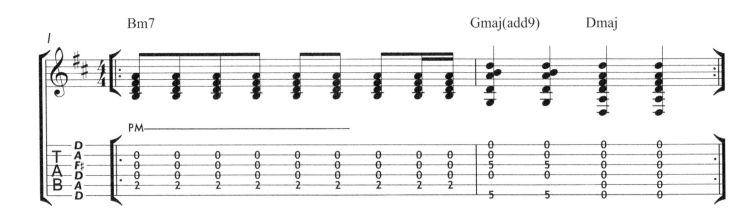

Phoebe Bridgers

American indie-folk artist Phoebe Bridgers typifies the modern sound of the genre with melancholy lyrics and acoustic and electric guitars melded with electronic production. Collaborations with artists including Taylor Swift, Ryan Adams and The 1975 have helped bring her music to a wider rock/pop audience. Her guitar work veers between traditional folk/americana approaches in standard tuning, and richer altered tunings, largely driven by her admiration of Elliott Smith.

Let's begin with Bridger's more traditional folk/americana approach to embellishing chords. This progression is I IV V in G Major (G – C – D) but she uses Csus2 and Dsus4 chords to create a modern sound.

These parts sound better with a capo on the higher frets, as the open position can get a bit muddy.

Example 5u

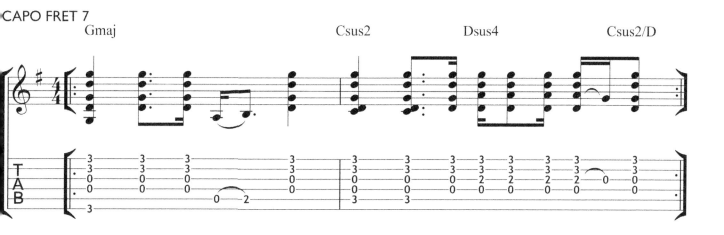

This next part features busier embellishments. Keep your third and fourth fingers fretted on the B and E strings throughout as these anchor the chords, around which your first finger hammers-on to the A and D strings.

Again, you can brighten the sound by playing higher on the neck with a capo.

Example 5v

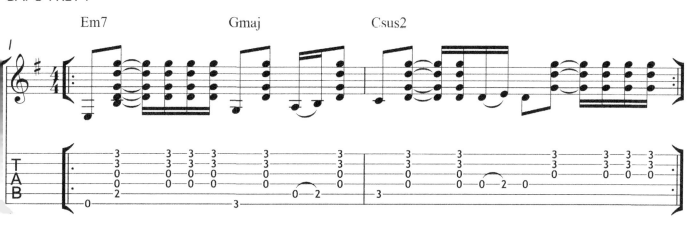

Re-tuning just one string can make chords easier to play and help you quickly find new sounds. Here, we drop the G string down a tone to F.

This idea is a moving bassline played against a static chord which creates a lot of colour. Use your thumb on the 1st fret of the E string, your second finger on the D string, and your first finger on the B string. The third finger takes care of the moving bass notes. On the recording, I emulate Bridger's modified "rubber bridge" guitar sound by inserting a simple pencil eraser under the bridge of a Jazzmaster.

Example 5w

D#ADGA#D is a close cousin of DADGAD, and its purpose is to use open strings to create some interesting chords. Start with your fourth finger on the E string and your third finger on the G string. From here, your first finger takes care of the E string in bar two, your second finger frets the A string in bar three, and your first finger takes care of the A string in bar four.

Example 5x

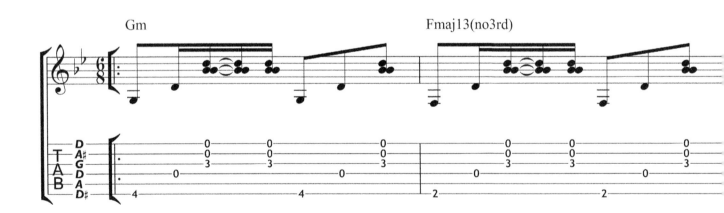

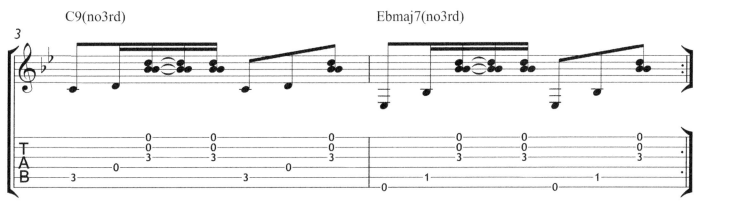

Finally, let's move down to CGCFAD tuning (also known as C6/9sus4 tuning). This is another example of how you can use a great chord voicing, unique to a tuning, and then move bass notes against it to outline a progression. Writing like this can be easier than trying to find fresh ideas in standard tuning and certainly gets you out of common ruts!

Example 5y

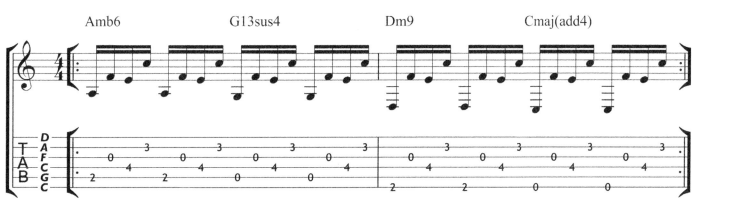

Chapter Six – Altered Tunings Part Two

In this final chapter, we'll explore those players who explore somewhat bespoke altered tunings. When we're learning, it can be tempting to ignore some of the more outlandish tunings due to the time it takes to tune the guitar to them. However, the more you use altered tunings the faster you'll become at accessing them, and the more you'll be inspired to explore them and develop your own tunings.

Nick Drake

Although he didn't achieve widespread success in his lifetime, English singer-songwriter Nick Drake's legacy and influence were pivotal. His pastoral sound gave folk guitar a new dimension, and his exploration of altered tunings (many of his own creation) gave his compositions a signature sound that can be hard to replicate. A deft fingerpicker, he's a required study for any guitarist looking for the roots of the indie-folk sound.

Some of Nick Drake's tunings were as extreme as BEBEBE, but he also occasionally used standard tuning, so we'll start there to help access his sound.

This example shows how he added colour to simple open chords. Play the Emaj(add9) chord with your second finger at the 2nd fret, your fourth finger at the 4th fret, and your third finger on the 1st fret of the G string. Release your third finger to play the gorgeous Emadd9 in the bar two.

Example 6a

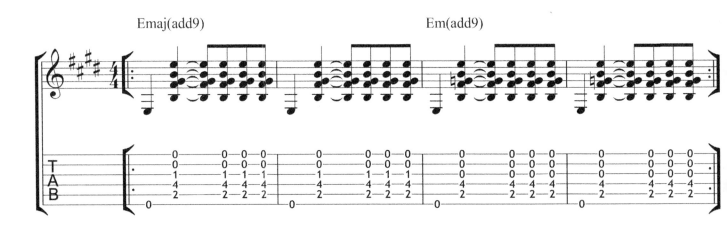

This Keith Richards style part moves to a rich E6sus chord in bar two. Start this example with your first finger barred across the D, G, and B strings, which facilitates a smooth move to the D in bar two. The E6sus4 is a bit of a stretch, so use your fourth finger on the A string, your first finger for the D string, and your third finger on the G string.

Example 6b

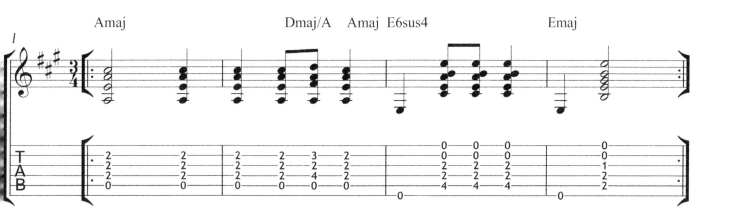

This example showcases Drake's deft fretting and picking hand work. While it looks daunting, it's based around chord shapes with some pull-offs within the chords. Keep the bassline as a solid pulse outlining the beat. The legato phrasing rides over the top, but ensure you stay in tempo – your thumb is your metronome! If the E major in bar one is new, try using your third finger at the 4th fret, your first finger at the 2nd fret, and your fourth finger at the 4th fret.

Example 6c

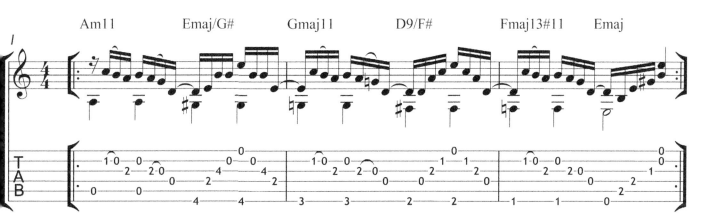

Now let's explore a common Nick Drake altered tuning of EADF#BE. It's close to standard tuning, so just lower the G string by a semitone. This classic folk fingerpicking pattern has an alternating bassline on the E and D strings with a syncopated melody over the top. In bar three, at the end of beat 3 you need to time the pull-off with your third finger at the 2nd fret to coincide with the open A string on beat 4.

Example 6d

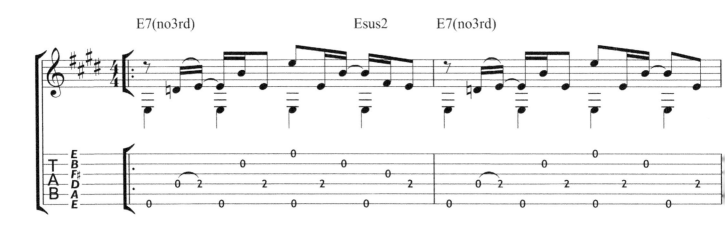

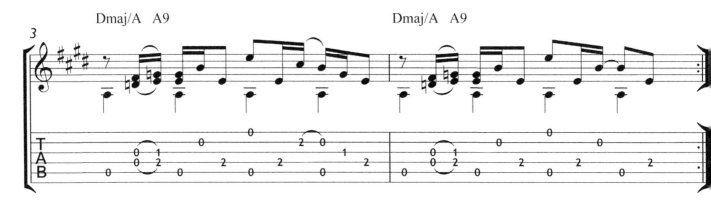

This example features a reverse roll that starts on the A string then picks back up from the B string. Many players default to picking downwards from the bass string, but reversing the pattern can create new ideas. In bar four, use your first finger at the 3rd fret and your fourth finger at the 6th fret, being careful that the underside of the finger doesn't touch the open G string.

Example 6e

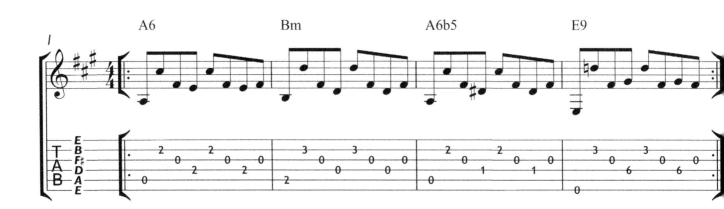

Elliott Smith

Indie-folk pioneer Elliott Smith tragically died in 2003 aged just 34, but left a legacy of six studio albums which are a blueprint for anyone wishing to study indie-folk guitar. Altered tunings, complex fingerpicking, and heavy electric guitar riffs all feature across his recorded output. Emerging at the tail end of the grunge scene, he was influenced by classic folk from Paul Simon and Leonard Cohen, alongside bands like The Beatles and Elvis Costello.

Smith developed an array of altered tunings, but he also wrote in standard and we'll start there with our exploration of his style.

This example features two simple chords, but the fingerpicking pattern and alternating bassline recreate his personal folk feel. Use the picking hand thumb on the low E and A strings, your second finger on the G, and your first finger on the D string.

Example 6f

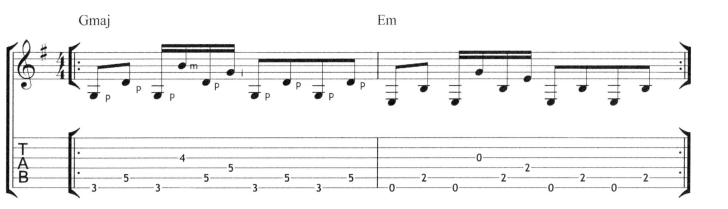

Plan your fretting fingering in advance before trying these gorgeous Elliott Smith chords. Begin bar one with your first finger on the 2nd fret and your third finger at the 3rd. To get to the Bmb6, keep your third finger in place, move your first finger to the 2nd fret of the A string, and add your fourth finger at the 4th fret. Your third finger stays in place throughout bar two, while your second finger takes care of the 3rd fret.

Example 6g

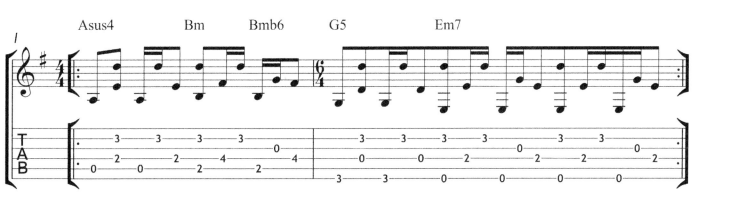

We move to open D Major tuning now (DADF#AD) where the open strings do most of the work to create these beautiful voicings. To avoid sounding the A string in bar three, fret the E string with your third finger at the 5th fret, then rest the underside of that finger against the A string to mute it. Build the rest of the chord with your second finger on the G string and your first finger on the B string.

Example 6h

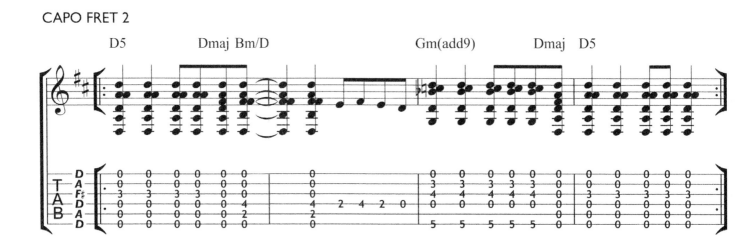

Here are some more lovely Elliott Smith chords in Open D, and again the open strings take care of most of the work. This example sounds great and demonstrates how often "less is more". Strum with a pick, and for the smoothest chord change use your first finger on the 3rd fret and follow this with your second finger in bar two.

Example 6i

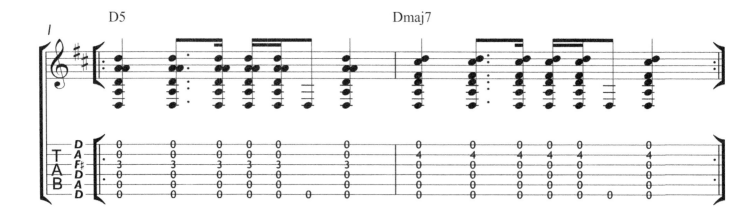

This example features a more complex fingerpicking example in Open D, so build this up one bar at a time as there's a lot going on.

In bar two, place a partial barre across the 5th fret on the top three strings and use your fourth finger on the 7th fret. To keep the strings ringing, your fourth finger should stay fretted while you add your third finger on the 7th fret.

Example 6j

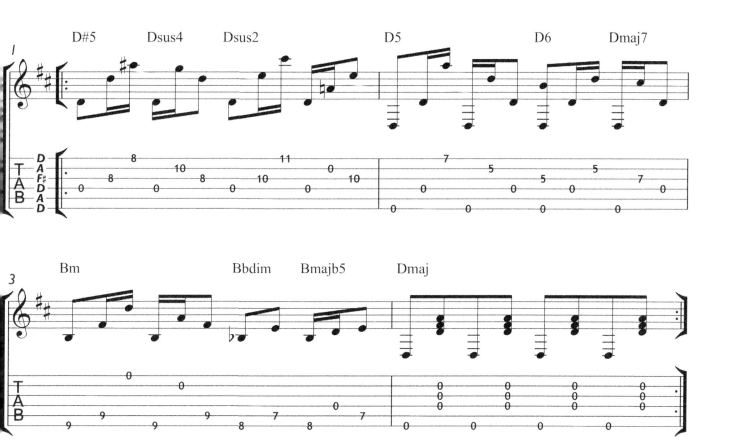

Jose Gonzales

Born in Sweden to Argentinian parents, Jose Gonzales' nylon string guitar work features complex rhythms with a world music and classical influence. Some of his primary influences are Latin folk musicians like Cuban singer-songwriter Silvio Rodriguez. Gonzales generally performs as a solo artist, creating deft fingerpicked parts which can be fairly challenging.

Studying Gonzales' classical/bossa nova based style is a workout for the picking hand, so let's start with an easy, rolling pattern, featuring a descending bassline on the E string. To pick the E, A and D strings, use your thumb on the E string, your first finger on the A and your second finger on the D. Halfway through bar three use your third finger for the G string.

Example 6k

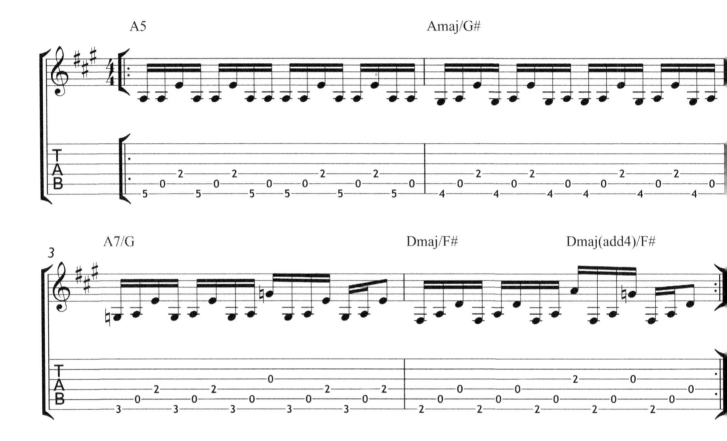

Gonzales' playing often includes challenging syncopations and the next few examples show you how to develop these.

Example 6l is a melodic line in Drop D tuning that sits over the alternating bassline in Example 6m. Use your first, second and third fingers to pick the top three strings. In the fretting hand, use your second finger on the B string and your fourth finger on the G string for reasons that will become apparent in a moment!

Example 6l

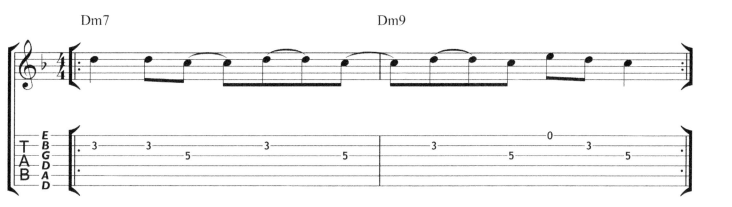

Here is the bassline that accompanies the previous example. Tune the low E string down to Drop D and use the picking hand thumb on each note. So far, no great challenge... until you put it all together!

Example 6m

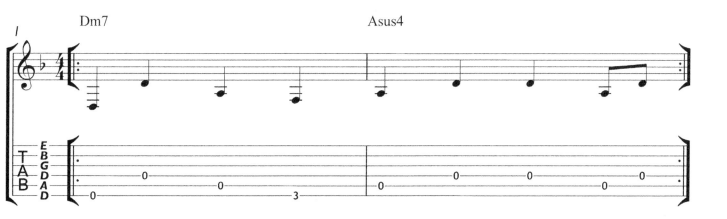

When we put both parts together, the syncopation of the melody against the bassline immediately becomes apparent (and challenging!) Use the same fingering as before for the melody, and your first finger for the 3rd fret of the low E string. Ensure you can play the bassline as a steady pulse of "1 2 3 4" before you introduce the melody over the top.

Example 6n

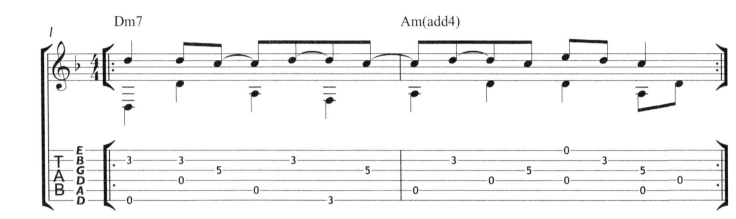

From Drop D, tune the the G string down a semitone to F# to create a beautiful D6/9 tuning (DADF#BE).

Use this tuning to play these Gonzales-style chords. As with the Elliott Smith examples, though they are simple to play, they sound amazing!

Example 6o

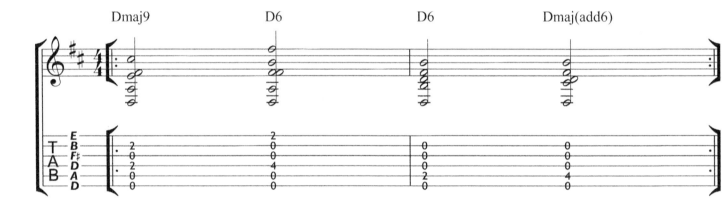

Bon Iver

Bon Iver's 2007 release, *For Emma, Forever Ago,* is a seminal work in the indie-folk genre. Founder Justin Vernon started as a solo act under the Bon Iver name and recorded *For Emma* alone in 2006. His main influences are Bob Dylan, americana legend John Prine, and indie stalwarts The Indigo Girls. Vernon is another player with a unique guitar style, based around his own tunings and extensive capo use.

This standard tuning example uses a flamenco-inspired strum and slap technique. Use your picking hand fingers to brush down the strings on beat 1, then slap the body of the guitar with your palm on beat 2. After the slap, rake back up the strings with the first finger of your picking hand. Listen closely to the audio to capture the feel.

Example 6p

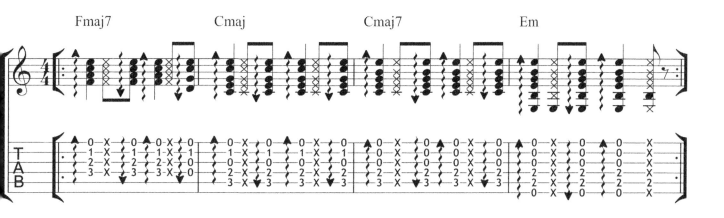

Here's an example where basic chords are enriched with colourful add9, add11 and 6sus4 variants. Planning your fretting fingerings is essential here, so use your first finger on the A string, your fourth finger on the G string, and your second finger on the B string. On beat 3 of bar two, move your first finger over to the low E string while keeping your other fingers in place.

Example 6q

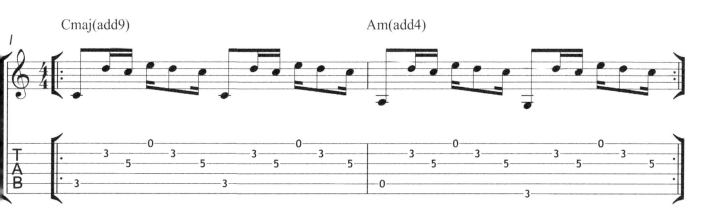

Tune the low E string down a tone to D here and strum this example with a pick. To play the F#m11 in bar one, barre the 4th fret with your first finger, use your fourth finger at the 7th fret, and your second at the 5th. The "X"s indicate guitar body slaps as above, but this time slap with the heel of your strumming hand.

Example 6r

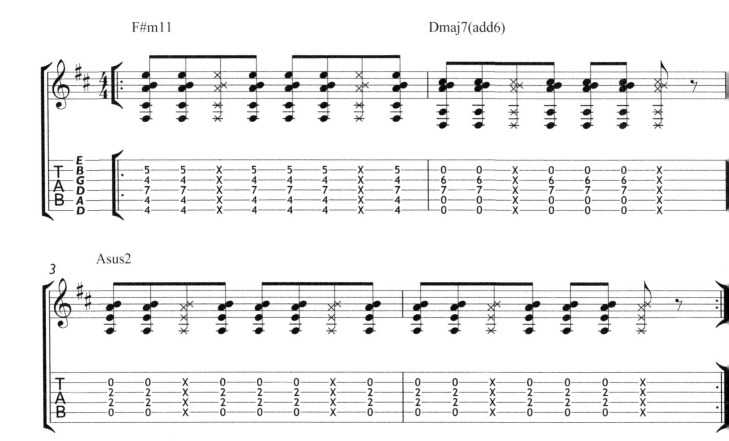

A basic Em – A major – D major chord progression sounds beautiful in Open D tuning (DADF#AD). Try strumming this with a light pick, and in bar one use your second finger on the E string, third finger on the A string, and first finger on the G string at the 1st fret.

Example 6s

CAPO FRET 7

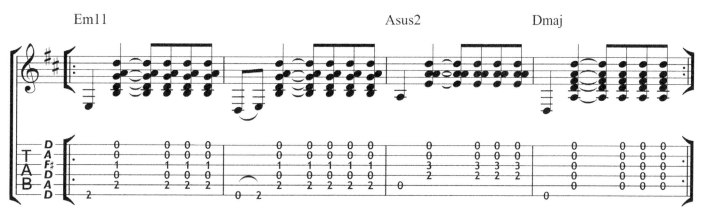

To tune to DAC#EAD from the previous example, lower the D (4th string) by a semitone and the G string down by a tone.

In this example, the E at the 3rd fret of the D string remains in place as a *pedal* while everything else moves against it. In bar one, your second finger plays the 3rd fret, and your fourth finger plays the 4th on the G string. Use your third finger on the E string and your first finger at the 2nd fret in bar two.

Example 6t

CAPO FRET 4

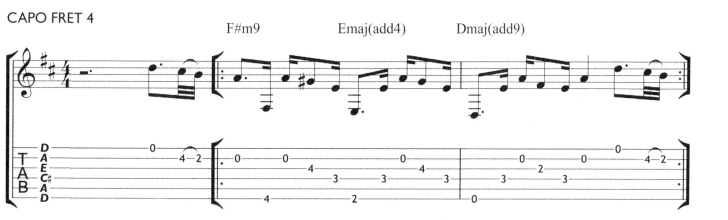

Ben Howard

Like Nick Drake, English singer-songwriter Ben Howard uses an array of unusual altered tunings, inspired by Joni Mitchell among others. Howard's music features rich chords that are only accessible in his bespoke tunings and he creates John Martyn-like, effects-laden soundscapes with fingerpicking and strumming.

Ben Howard also uses standard tuning, so we'll start there with an example that combines syncopation and a moving bassline. The rhythmic pattern is challenging but when you've nailed it in bar one, the same pattern continues. In bar two, keep your fourth finger at the 3rd fret, then use your first finger at the 1st fret, followed by your third finger in bar three.

Example 6u

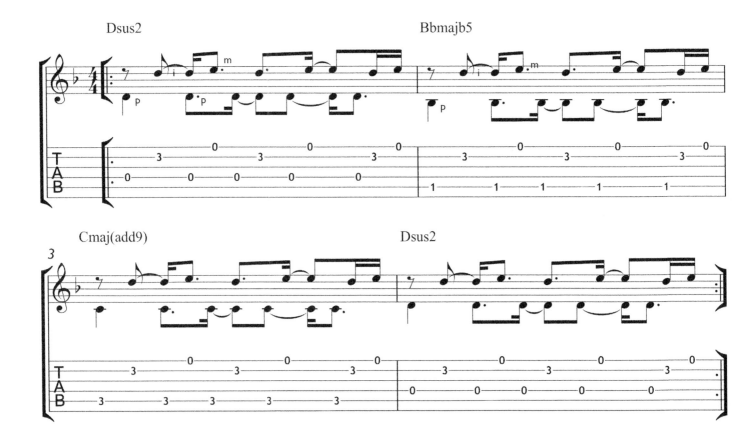

This Drop D example keeps the rhythmic pattern you've just used but with more fretting finger movements.

In the first two bars use your third finger on the A string, your fourth finger on the B string, and your first finger at the 9th fret before moving it to the 10th fret of the B string. In the third bar use your third finger at the 7th fret of the B string and your second finger on the 6th fret of the G string.

Example 6v

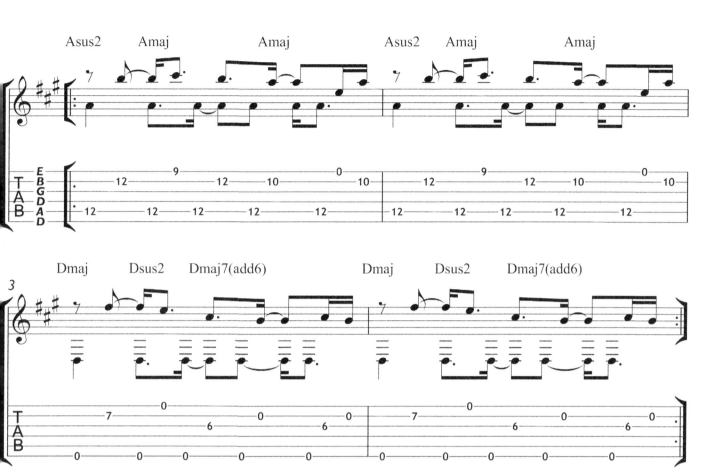

Re-tune to EADGAD now, a close cousin of DADGAD.

Most players always play bass notes on the beat, but notice how Howard syncopates the open A string so that he plays it on beats one and two, but then plays it on the last 1/16th note of beat two, the "&" of beat three, and the second 1/16th note of beat four. Learn this bassline on its own before adding the melody on top (which is also syncopated!)

Example 6w

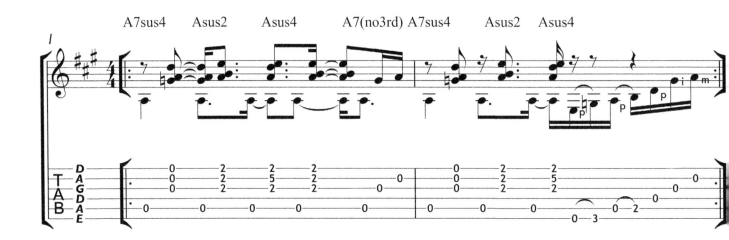

Here's a more straightforward, traditional folk picking pattern that demonstrates some great sounds in EADGAD tuning.

Ben Howard sometimes uses chords with more challenging fingerings and here is an example of that approach.

In bars two and three, use your second finger for any notes at the 3rd fret and your second finger for those on the 2nd. In bar four, play the hammer-on/pull-off lick with your first and third fingers.

Example 6x

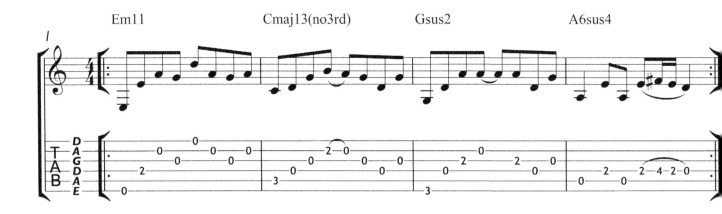

Here are some more great chords in EADGAD. Once again, the fingerings should be mapped out in advance. In bars one and two use your first finger on the A string, your second finger on the G string, and your third finger on the B string. In bar three, use your third finger on the low E string, your first finger on the G string, and your second finger on the B string.

Example 6y

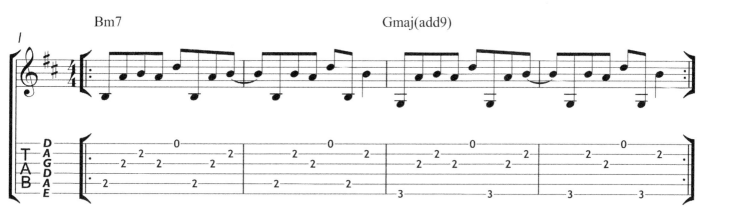

Chapter 7 – Performance Piece

To conclude our indie-folk journey, here is a final performance piece to remind us how we can colour simple chord progressions by getting creative with chord voicings. All the chords here belong to the key of G Major, but instead of playing in the open position we're using shapes high up the neck, which contrast nicely with the lower sound of the open strings. This juxtaposition of high and low lets us extract some interesting textures from the guitar and a few fingering changes reveal a host of possibilities.

This piece is played with a capo at the 2nd fret. The capo serves two functions here: to raise the pitch and therefore brighten the sound of the chords, and also to lower the action slightly higher up the neck to make things easier on the fretting hand. You can, of course, just follow the TAB and play the tune without a capo, but you'll need it if you want to play along with the recording.

To begin with, familiarise yourself with the fretting hand shapes. The chords are generally based around an open position C major shape. The defining feature of this piece is the common tones shared by all the chord voicings, located at the 8th fret of the B string and the 10th fret of the E string. Although some of the chord shapes may look daunting at first glance, when you have these common tones in place they act as an anchor, around which everything else moves, so start by fretting these two notes when working out your fingerings.

Use the first finger at the 8th fret of the B string, and the fourth finger at the 10th fret of the E string. For any notes at the 9th fret use your second finger, and for anything at the 10th fret use the third finger. There is one slight twist! We don't have enough fingers to play the Cmaj9 shapes here, so you'll need to hook your thumb over the 8th fret to play the bass note for that chord, while keeping all your remaining fingers fretted. This may feel awkward initially, but if you adjust your wrist position slightly, you'll be able to do it. This is probably the hardest shape to play here, but it shows how the idiosyncrasies of indie-folk lead to some great (though challenging) sounds!

The rhythm remains the same throughout, so you can focus on your fretting hand. There are several points at which the chord changes on the last 1/16th note of a bar, so that it lands just before beat 1 of the next bar (known as a "pushed" chord). The first example of this is the Cmaj9 at the end of bar four. Look through the whole piece and identify the pushed chords, so they don't take you by surprise when they come up.

When you've learned this piece, experiment and try moving other simple open position shapes up the neck to see what sounds you can create against the open strings. Then, make some fingering changes within the chord shape to see what else is revealed. There's a whole world of great chords waiting to be discovered when you take this approach!

Example 7a

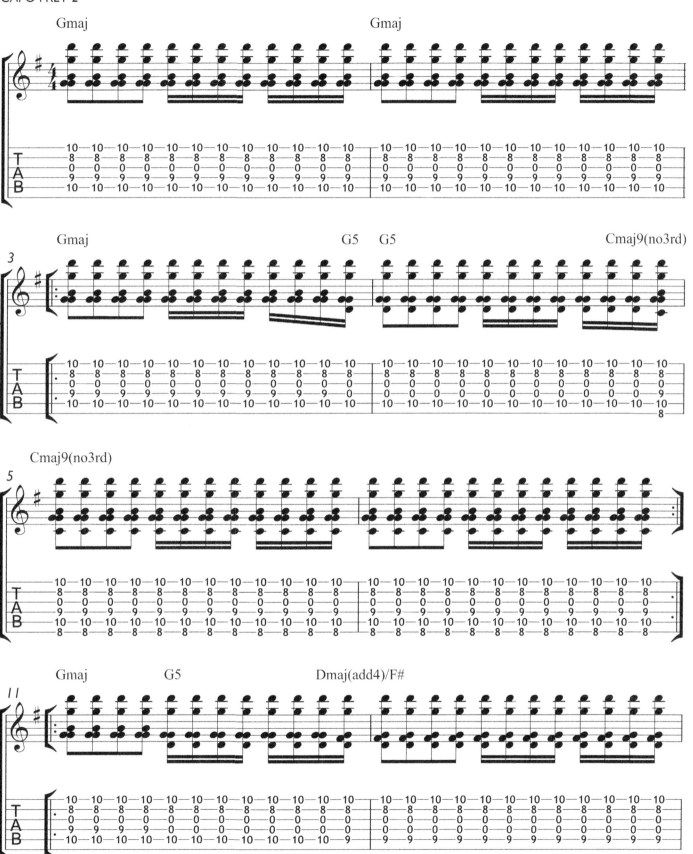

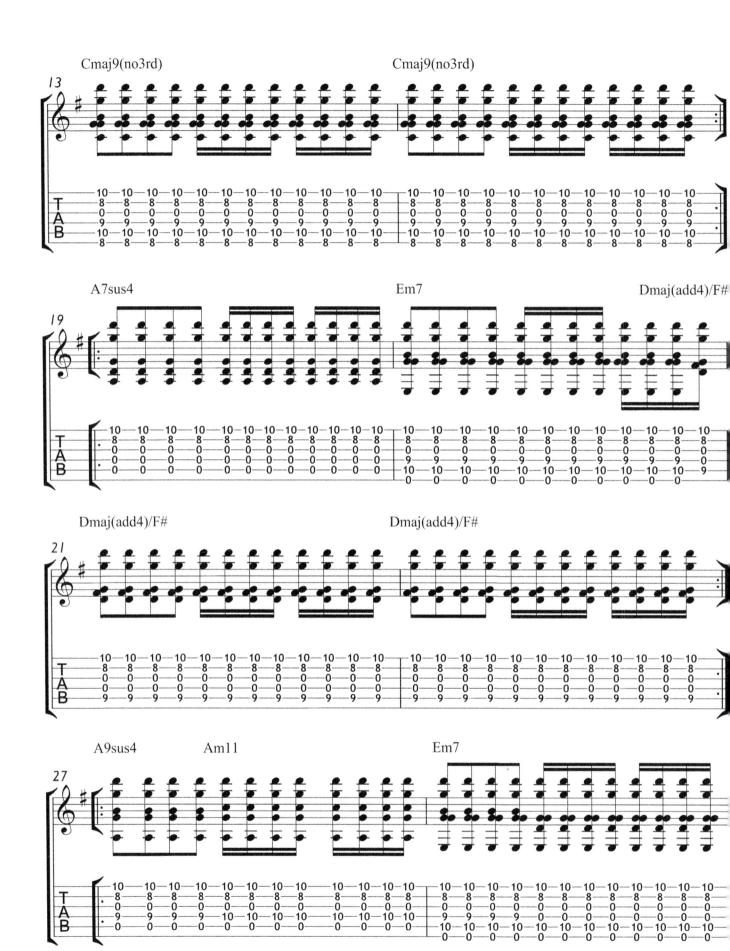

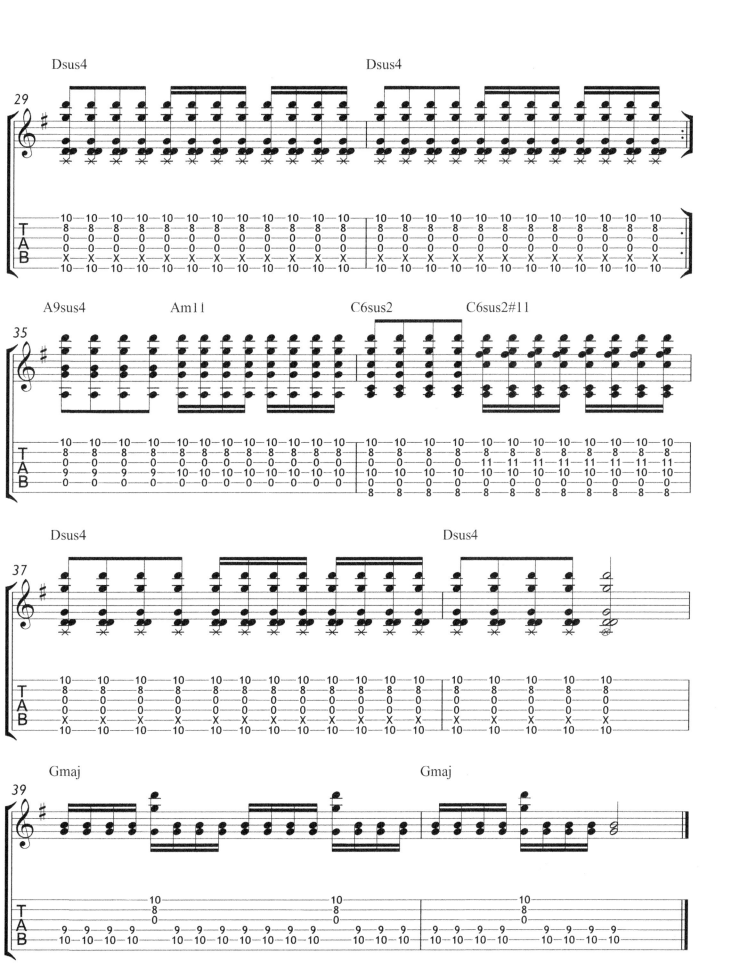

Conclusion

I hope you've enjoyed this journey through the rich, creative world of indie folk guitar. Hopefully the idiosyncrasies of the players we've looked at will inspire you to approach your guitar in a different way. It's easy to become overwhelmed with a genre like indie folk, as there are so many players with so many varied approaches. A good starting point is to identify four or five artists who particularly resonate with you, then isolate a few tracks from each for detailed study. It's always best to transcribe material for yourself (rather than buying a book of the songs), as this will help you get much deeper into their music.

Altered tunings can be a lifetime's study and I'd recommend working on a handful of tunings that really speak to you at first. Get familiar with some basic chord shapes and scales in each tuning, learn how the tenth intervals lay out on the neck, and take it from there. Some of the more extreme tunings yield a wide range of great ideas, while you might only explore others when you are learning a specific artist's repertoire.

As with everything, the more you explore a tuning, the more you'll find yourself falling into familiar shapes and ruts. If this happens, try de-tuning one string to move you away from your comfort zone and you'll be finding new ideas again before you know it.

Have fun with this style and make it your own!

Printed in Great Britain
by Amazon

47203095R00057